VARIATION

1. a) George describes himself as 2.01m tall, blue eyes, blonde hair, a scar, speaks german and is a bit overweight at 1200N.

   Say whether these features are genetic, environmental or a combination of both.

   b) Give three examples of environmental causes of variation and three examples of genetic causes of variation.

2. a) What is a mutation?

   b) Cancer is caused by a mutation that leads to cells growing and multiplying out of control. The cells no longer function properly. Explain why people are concerned about prolonged sunbathing and a thinner ozone layer.

   c) A footballer is taken to hospital with a suspected broken femur (bone in top part of the leg). Explain why the radiologist places a thin sheet of lead over his reproductive organs prior to taking an X-ray.

3. Explain why sexual reproduction causes variation.

---- HIGHER TIER ----

4. a) 'A person can be taught to draw but a truly great artist is born.' Use your knowledge of the effects of inheritance and environment to discuss whether the above statement is correct.

   b) State one genetic and one environmental factor which could affect a person's health.

GENE STRUCTURE AND MUTATION

Variation, Inheritance And Evolution

2

1. a) Explain, as fully as you can, what genes are.

   b) What are chromosomes?

   c) How many chromosomes are found in human skin cells?

   d) How many chromosomes are found in sperm cells?

   HIGHER TIER

2. A DNA molecule consists of two strands linked together. Describe, with the help of a diagram, how they are linked.

3. Explain, in your own words, how genes work.

4. a) What are mutations?

   b) Describe, using diagrams to help, how a mutation results in the production of a different sequence of amino acids in a protein.

CELL DIVISION

Variation, Inheritance And Evolution

HIGHER TIER

1. Connect the words MEIOSIS and MITOSIS to the correct statements.

   MITOSIS — MEIOSIS

   - Cell Division
   - Involved in asexual reproduction
   - Produces cells with the same number of chromosomes
   - Involved in sexual reproduction
   - Produces gametes with half the number of chromosomes
   - Produces genetically identical clones
   - Increases variation in offspring

2. a) The following statements refer to mitosis. Complete the explanation by drawing a diagram to support each statement.

   | Parent cell with two pairs of chromosomes. | Each chromosome replicates itself. | The cell divides for the only time. | Genetically identical daughter cells are formed. |

   b) Why must meiosis occur before fertilisation?

3. a) 'Sexual reproduction promotes variation'. Explain how this happens.

   b) Why is increased variation an advantage to a species?

THE TERMINOLOGY OF INHERITANCE

Variation, Inheritance And Evolution — 4

HIGHER TIER

1. Insert the missing words into the following passage ...

   In eye colour, the .... for blue eyes is .... to the .... for brown eyes. Because brown is .... to blue, an individual who has both genes will still have .... eyes, even though he is carrying a blue .... Only if an individual has two .... will they have blue eyes.

2. a) T is the allele for tongue rolling and t is the allele for non-tongue rolling. State whether the following can roll their tongues or not.

   i) tt ....
   ii) TT ....
   iii) tT ....
   iv) Tt ....

   b) B is the allele for brown eyes and b is the allele for blue eyes. State the colour of the following people's eyes.

   i) Bb ....
   ii) bb ....
   iii) bB ....
   iv) BB ....

3. a) Judy Smith has brown eyes, her husband Tony also has brown eyes. Their daughter Poppy however has blue eyes. Complete the diagram to show how Poppy inherited blue eyes.

   JUDY SMITH   X   TONY SMITH

   PARENTS' ALLELES:

   ALLELES IN SPERM AND EGG:

   ALLELES IN POPPY SMITH:

   b) From this information we can say that ...
   (i) Judy Smith is .... for eye colour.
   (ii) Tony Smith is .... for eye colour.
   (iii) Poppy Smith is .... for eye colour.

4. State whether the following combinations of genes are HOMOZYGOUS DOMINANT, HETEROZYGOUS or HOMOZYGOUS RECESSIVE.

   i) Tt ....
   ii) BB ....
   iii) ee ....
   iv) Bb ....
   v) EE ....
   vi) tT ....

MONOHYBRID INHERITANCE

Variation, Inheritance And Evolution

5

HIGHER TIER

1. Complete the **TWO** different crosses between a brown-eyed and a blue-eyed parent.

   BROWN EYES × BLUE EYES   BROWN EYES × BLUE EYES

   PARENTS: BB × bb   Bb × bb

   GAMETES:

   OFFSPRING:

2. Explain how parents with brown eyes could produce children with blue eyes. Use a diagram to help you.

3. a) Complete the following diagrams to show how attached and unattached ear lobes might be inherited. (Unattached are dominant.)

   Ee × Ee   Ee × ee   ee × ee

   b) What are the percentage chances of producing individuals with attached ear lobes in each of the three cases above.

   (i) ....
   (ii) ....
   (iii) ....

4. A homozygous tongue roller mates with a homozygous non-tongue roller. Their child mates with a heterozygous partner. Draw a genetic diagram to show the probable ratios produced and use genetic terminology to describe the gene combinations of the offspring. (Tongue rolling is dominant).

OCR Reference: Page 8   *Lonsdale* Science Revision Guides - OCR Science: Phase 2

INHERITANCE OF SEX/INHERITED AND INFECTIOUS DISEASES

Variation, Inheritance And Evolution

HIGHER TIER

1. Complete the following diagram showing how the sex of a child depends on the sex chromosomes the child inherits.

   MALE → ☐ ☐   FEMALE → ☐ ☐

   SEX CHROMOSOMES IN SPERM   SEX CHROMOSOMES IN EGGS

   SEX CHROMOSOMES IN CHILDREN ....

   SEX OF CHILDREN ....

2. a) What are the chances of a woman having FOUR consecutive male children?

   b) What are the chances of a woman having FIVE consecutive female children?

3. a) What is cystic fibrosis?

   b) What is sickle cell anaemia?

   HIGHER TIER

   c) In parts of West Africa there is a greater proportion of people with sickle cell anaemia. Explain Why.

4. With the aid of a diagram explain how a couple, neither of whom have cystic fibrosis, could have a child with cystic fibrosis.

CLONING TECHNIQUES IN PLANTS

Variation, Inheritance And Evolution — 7

1. a) What is the key characteristic of a plant obtained by asexual reproduction?

b) Why could this be desirable for commercial plant growers?

c) Give two examples of plants which can reproduce asexually.

i)

ii)

2. a) Discuss the advantages and disadvantages of commercially cloning plants.

b) When a gardener has a plant with all the desired characteristics he may decide to produce many of them by taking cuttings. Explain how the gardener should do this.

3. a) What is a clone?

── HIGHER TIER ──

b) Explain how clones may be produced using tissue culture.

4. Cloning is an issue which arouses fierce debate. In the space below outline some of the arguments for and against this biological technique.

OCR Reference: Page 10 — Lonsdale Science Revision Guides - OCR Science: Phase 2

SELECTIVE BREEDING

Variation, Inheritance And Evolution — 8

1. Present day wheat farmers would not readily recognise the wheat plants from many hundreds of years ago.

   Wheat plant from hundreds of years ago.

   Modern day wheat plant

   a) What are the main advantages of the modern day wheat plant over its predecessor?

   b) State ONE additional characteristic that would be useful for modern day wheat plants to possess.

   c) Explain, in as much detail as possible, how the modern wheat plant was developed.

2. Use your imagination to dream up two completely new varieties of organisms that you think could possibly be produced by selective breeding, and would be useful in modern farming. Try to make your new varieties as believable as possible (i.e. NOT a Tandoori chicken!).

   i)

   ii)

   —— HIGHER TIER ——

3. a) State two advantages of selective breeding.

   i)

   ii)

   b) State two disadvantages of selective breeding.

   i)

   ii)

4. Selective breeding is responsible for the huge number of varieties of pedigree dogs which exist. Discuss whether this is an acceptable use of selective breeding.

GENETIC ENGINEERING

Variation, Inheritance And Evolution — HIGHER TIER

1. Give **FOUR** examples of the genetic modification of organisms.

2. Explain how genes can be used to protect soya plants against insect damage.

3. a) Describe how large quantities of insulin can be produced by genetic engineering.

   b) What are the advantages of obtaining insulin by genetic engineering instead of using insulin extracted from the pancreas of pigs?

   c) It is already possible to control the sex of an unborn baby. Do you think parents should be able to design their baby by selecting its genetic make-up? Explain your answer.

   d) Discuss the advantages and risks of genetic engineering.

EVOLUTION, EXTINCTION AND THE FOSSIL RECORD

Variation, Inheritance And Evolution — **10**

1. a) What is evolution?

b) What does 'extinct' mean?

2. a) Give FOUR different reasons why a species may become extinct.

(i)
(ii)
(iii)
(iv)

b) The Dodo is now extinct but used to live on an island in the Indian Ocean. The Dodo was a large flightless bird that fed on seeds. The Dodo had lived on the island for many thousands of years before European sailors introduced monkeys and pigs to the island. Monkeys eat leaves, fruits and birds' eggs. Pigs dig down to the roots of plants which they then eat.
Explain, as fully as you can, why the Dodo became extinct.

c) The number of native British Red Squirrels has decreased significantly since the introduction of the much larger Grey Squirrel about one hundred years ago. Give some possible reasons for this.

3. a) What are fossils and how are they formed?

b) How do fossils provide evidence for evolution?

Lonsdale Science Revision Guides - OCR Science: Phase 2 — OCR Reference: Page 13

EVOLUTION BY NATURAL SELECTION

Variation, Inheritance And Evolution

HIGHER TIER

1. Describe the key observations which led Darwin to his theory of evolution.

2. a) Explain the significance of each of these FOUR factors for evolution by Natural Selection.

   STAGE 1: VARIATION

   STAGE 2: COMPETITION

   STAGE 3: BEST ADAPTED

   STAGE 4: PASSING ON OF GENES

   b) Warfarin is a poison that was used to kill rats. An increasing number of rats are now warfarin resistant. Explain how this could have happened.

   c) Explain the evolution of penicillin-resistant bacteria.

4. Why did Darwin's theory meet with a hostile reaction in some quarters?

STRUCTURE OF A FLOWERING PLANT

The Working Plant — 1

1. Two of the main organs of a flowering plant are named in the table below.
   For each organ name its main component(s) and state its function(s).

ORGAN	MAIN COMPONENT(S)	FUNCTION(S)
Stem	1.	1.
	2.	2. Transports water and minerals from roots to leaves.
Leaves	1.	1.

2. a) State TWO functions of the roots.

   i) ....

   ii) ....

   b) What is the function of the flower?

   ....

3. a) Explain how water and minerals get from the soil around a plant to the leaves of the plant.

   ....

   b) Explain what translocation is.

   ....

4. Complete the crossword below, the number of letters are shown after the clues.

ACROSS
1. Movement of food substances around the plant (13)
2. A function of the roots (9)
3. These absorb water (5)
7. Carried out in the leaf (14)
10. Reproductive organs are required to make these (5)
12. The stem provides a system of _____ (9)

DOWN
1. Movement of water from roots to leaves (13)
4. The reproductive organs are found here (6)
5. Transports water and minerals (5)
6. Transports food substances (6)
8. A function of the stem (7)
9. Absorbed by the leaf for photosynthesis (8)
11. A characteristic of leaves (5)

THE PROCESS OF PHOTOSYNTHESIS

The Working Plant — 2

1. **Glucose can be used by plants for energy or to build up bigger molecules.**

   The diagram shows a starch molecule. The part labelled A is a glucose molecule.

   STARCH

   a) What is the name of the process which produces glucose in a plant?

   b) Name the process which uses glucose to produce energy for the plant.

   c) How does the plant store the products of photosynthesis?

2. a) **Write the word equation for photosynthesis.**

   b) A leaf from a variegated plant is shown below. The plant was left in sunlight and then tested for starch.

   (i) Which part of the leaf (green or white) will have starch present?

   (ii) Explain your answer to part (i).

   — White area
   — Green area

3. a) **Starch is a large molecule made from glucose. Cellulose and protein are also large molecules made from glucose. For each one state what they are used for in the plant.**

   starch:
   cellulose:
   protein:

   b) Describe how protein is produced from glucose.

   c) If a plant was short of protein, what effect would it have on the plant?

   d) In what form is the energy produced by green plants stored in the seeds?

   e) Explain why it is important for plants to convert sugars into starch for storage.

OCR Reference: Page 17 — Lonsdale Science Revision Guides - OCR Science: Phase 2

FACTORS AFFECTING THE RATE OF PHOTOSYNTHESIS • The Working Plant — 3

1. a) Describe how you would expect the rate of photosynthesis to be affected by each of the four seasons of the year.

   i) SPRING:

   ii) SUMMER:

   iii) AUTUMN:

   iv) WINTER:

   b) Explain how a gardener could increase the rate of photosynthesis of his plants.

============ HIGHER TIER ============

2. A student decided that he would test a green plant to see how the rate of photosynthesis changed with temperature. The results he obtained are shown below.

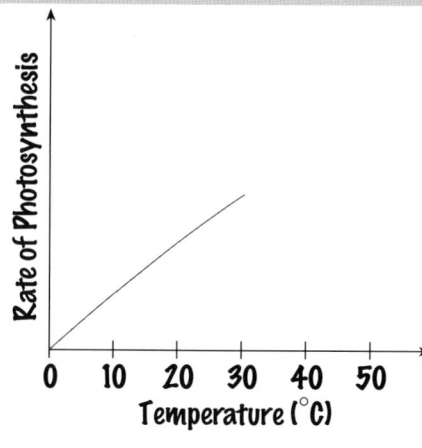

   a) He did not finish the experiment. Can you sketch on the graph the results he might have obtained?

   b) Explain why photosynthesis varies with temperature over a range from 0°C to 50°C.

3. The graph shows how the rate of photosynthesis changed on two different days.

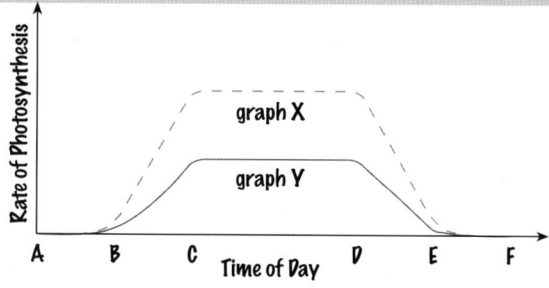

   a) Which graph, X or Y, represents a hot sunny day?

   b) Mark a D on the graph when dawn would occur and an N when nightfall occurs.

   c) Describe in detail what the graphs tell you about changes in photosynthesis throughout the day.

HOW THE LEAF IS ADAPTED FOR PHOTOSYNTHESIS • The Working Plant — 4

1. **Write down 4 ways in which a leaf is adapted for photosynthesis.**
   In each case explain how the adaptation benefits the leaf.

   a)

   b)

   c)

   d)

---- HIGHER TIER ----

2. **The diagram below shows the cellular structure of the leaf. Explain 4 ways in which the cellular structure is adapted for photosynthesis.**

   a)

   b)

   c)

   d)

TRANSPIRATION

The Working Plant — 5

1. a) By which process do plants lose water vapour from their leaves?

b) The diagram shows a cross-section of a leaf. Describe how the leaf is adapted to prevent water loss.

2. There are TWO separate transport systems in flowering plants. What are they called and what do they do?

(i)

(ii)

3. The diagram shows an experiment investigating the water uptake by a plant. The results table is shown below.

TIME FROM START (DAYS)	VOLUME OF WATER IN CYLINDER (cm³)
0	50
1	47
2	43
3	42
4	40

a) Why is a layer of oil placed in the measuring cylinder?

b) What has happened to the volume of water in the measuring cylinder?

c) How would you expect the results to have changed if ...

(i) ... the plant had been in a colder room?

(ii) ... the plant had been in a more humid atmosphere?

(iii) ... air had been blown over the leaves of the plant?

---- HIGHER TIER ----

4. 'Water loss by transpiration must happen during photosynthesis.' Explain this statement.

DIFFUSION AND OSMOSIS

The Working Plant — 6

1. a) Explain what is meant by the term 'diffusion'.

   b) Give an example of diffusion occurring in plants.

HIGHER TIER

2. a) What is meant by the term 'osmosis'?

   b) The diagram below shows an experiment to demonstrate osmosis. Explain the results in detail.

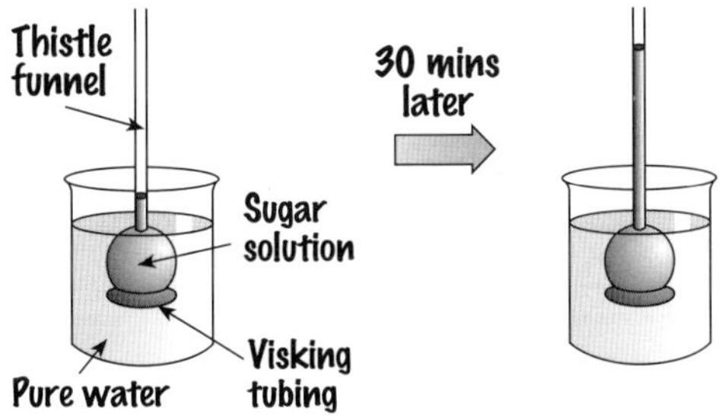

   Thistle funnel, Sugar solution, Visking tubing, Pure water — 30 mins later

   c) Which of the following are examples of osmosis? (✓ or ✗)

   Water evaporating from leaves.

   Water moving from plant cell to plant cell.

   Mixing pure water and sugar solution.

   Ink spreading through water.

   A pear losing water in a concentrated salt solution.

   Water moving from blood to body cells.

   Sugar absorbed from the intestine into the blood.

3. Nadia lives by the sea. Occasionally her garden is flooded by the sea water. Afterwards the plants in her garden wilt and die. Explain why flooding with sea water causes the plants to wilt.

4. Root hair cells absorb water from the soil. Describe how this happens.

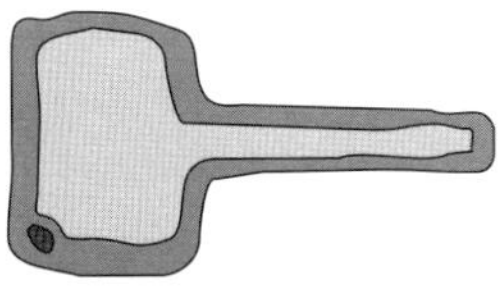

OCR Reference: Page 21

WATER LOSS AND WILTING

The Working Plant — 7

1. A student did an experiment to see what happened to a young plant when it was deprived of water. The plant was placed in a pot and left in a warm room for a few days without being watered.

Appearance of plant at start

Appearance of plant after a few days

a) Explain in detail:
   (i) how plants lose water.

   (ii) why the plant looks like this after a few days.

b) (i) Explain what a plant can do to reduce water loss.

   (ii) As a result of the plant reducing water loss, what other process will be slowed down?

   HIGHER TIER

   (iii) Explain why this process is slowed down when water loss is reduced.

   (iv) Which cells are responsible for controlling the size of the stomata?

c) Broad-leaved plants lose their leaves in winter, apply your knowledge of water loss and wilting to explain why this is a good survival strategy.

2. Water constantly moves into plant cells, assuming of course that there is plenty in the soil. This increases the turgor pressure.

   a) How does this help the plant?

   b) What stops the cells bursting?

PLANT MINERAL REQUIREMENTS

The Working Plant — 8

1. A group of scientists investigated the effect of the mass of fertiliser used on the yield of barley. They planted five fields of barley, added differing amounts of fertiliser to each field and five months later measured the amount of barley produced on each field. The results are shown in the table below.

Fertiliser added (kg)	Yield of Barley (tonnes)
0	18
50	27
100	34
150	38
200	38

a) Draw a bar graph to show the results.

b) State TWO variables the scientists must control to ensure a fair test.

i) .... ii) ....

c) Which of the above fields was used as a 'control'?

d) What yield of barley would have been produced by **75kg** of fertiliser?

e) What yield of barley would have been produced by **250kg** of fertiliser?

f) Explain fully the results obtained by the scientists.

HIGHER TIER

2. a) What is meant by a 'concentration gradient'?

b) What is meant by 'active transport'?

c) Explain why a root hair cell must absorb ions by active transport.

OCR Reference: Page 23

EXCHANGE OF GASES DURING BREATHING

Health In The Balance 1

1. Complete the crossword below:

ACROSS
2. This gas makes up 78% of the atmosphere and is inert (8)
3. and 1. This gas increases from 0.03% to 4% in exhaled air (6) and (7)

DOWN
4. An inert gas which makes up less than 1% of the atmosphere (5)
5. A gas necessary for life (6)
6. These gases don't react with anything (5)

2. Exhaled air contains an increased amount of water vapour and is warmer.

   a) Why does it contain more water vapour?

   b) Why is it warmer?

---- HIGHER TIER ----

3. Complete the following passage by filling in the missing words.

.... is produced during respiration but can't be allowed to accumulate in the blood because in high concentration it is .... Consequently, high levels of .... are detected by the ...., which then sends .... to the muscles between the .... and in the .... which cause the breathing rate to .... This removes .... via the lungs until it is at a suitably low concentration.

4. Why would re-breathing exhaled air cause the breathing rate to increase?

AEROBIC RESPIRATION

Health In The Balance 2

1. **a) How does the circulatory system ensure that the working cells in the body have enough energy?**

b) How is this affected by exercise?

c) What happens to the breathing rate during exercise?

2. **a) What is the difference between breathing and respiration?**

b) Write a word equation for aerobic respiration.

c) Isaac is running a long-distance race. A graph of his heart rate is shown below. What happens to Isaac's heart rate when he starts running the race?

d) What will happen to Isaac's breathing rate?

e) Use your knowledge of aerobic respiration to explain your answers.

f) Catherine was competing in a long-distance race, during which her blood glucose level dropped. Use your knowledge of respiration to explain how this would have stopped Catherine competing at her most efficient level.

OCR Reference: Page 26 — Lonsdale Science Revision Guides - OCR Science: Phase 2 — 21

ANAEROBIC RESPIRATION

Health In The Balance 3

1. Jane is playing football. She sprints the length of the field to score. She can barely celebrate because her legs have gone weak and rubbery and she can't get her breath back. Jane has just been respiring anaerobically.

   a) Write a word equation for this type of respiration.

   b) Explain, in as much detail as you can, why Jane's legs felt rubbery.

   c) Explain why Jane couldn't get her breath back to celebrate after she scored the goal.

   d) Explain why Jane cannot play all of the game at this rate.

   e) Why is aerobic respiration much more efficient than anaerobic respiration?

   f) Jane often does interval training. This involves jogging for 30 seconds, sprinting for 15 seconds, jogging for 30 seconds, sprinting for 15 seconds and so on.
      (i) Explain why Jane is **not** out of breath for the first 30 second jog.

      (ii) Explain why she **is** out of breath every time she jogs after sprinting.

----- HIGHER TIER -----

2. a) Explain what is meant by 'oxygen debt' and describe how it must be repaid.

   b) What happens to lactic acid in the tissues after exercise?

HOMEOSTASIS AND TEMPERATURE CONTROL

Health In The Balance — 4

1. a) Define homeostasis

   b) How does shivering help to raise body temperature?

   c) How does sweating help to reduce body temperature?

2. The temperature of the body has to be 'controlled'.

   a) What is normal body temperature?

   b) Why is this temperature maintained?

   ---- HIGHER TIER ----

   c) Which part of the body monitors temperature?

   d) The two diagrams below show a blood vessel and a sweat gland in the skin.

   A — SWEATING STOPPED, SWEAT GLAND, SHUNT VESSEL OPEN
   B — SWEAT, SWEAT GLAND, SHUNT VESSEL CLOSED

   (i) Which diagram, A or B, shows the skin in hot conditions?

   (ii) Explain in detail what happens when the body's temperature gets too low.

   (iii) Explain in detail what happens when the body gets too hot.

3. Explain in detail what is meant by the 'principle of negative feedback.'

OCR Reference: Page 28

CONTROL OF SALT, UREA & WATER CONTENT

Health In The Balance 5

1. a) Using the words from the word list label the following diagram.

Word list:
- Vena Cava
- Kidney
- Renal Vein
- Renal Artery
- Aorta
- Urethra
- Ureter
- Bladder
- Diaphragm

b) What is the function of the kidney?

c) Name three substances which, to differing degrees, are removed from the blood by the kidneys.

i)

ii)

iii)

--- HIGHER TIER ---

2. Kate had been cycling on a very hot day. Her urine was very yellow.

a) Why was her urine more yellow than normal?

b) How could she have prevented this?

c) Describe the body's response to falling blood water levels.

---

24 — Lonsdale Science Revision Guides - OCR Science: Phase 2 — OCR Reference: Page 29

DEFENCE AGAINST MICROBES

Health In The Balance — 6

1. Write down **THREE** ways in which the human body defends itself against disease.

   1. ....
   2. ....
   3. ....

2. a) During a recent outbreak of foot-and-mouth disease people who came into contact with it had to protect themselves from the human form of the disease. Suggest how they would have done this. (They needed to stop the microbes entering the body.)

   ....

   b) Explain why it is important to be particularly hygienic in hospital operating theatres.

   ....

   c) The diagram shows two cells which line the surface of breathing organs.
      (i) Describe how the mucus-secreting cell helps to protect the body from disease.

   ....

      (ii) Name **ONE** instance when excess mucus is produced.

   ....

   MUCUS-SECRETING CELL   CILIATED EPITHELIAL CELL

3. Name two ways in which white blood cells deal with dangerous microbes

   (i) ....
   (ii) ....

4. Some diseases such as measles we get once and never get again. We have acquired a natural immunity to the disease.

   Explain what we mean by 'natural immunity.'

   ....

OCR Reference: Page 30 — Lonsdale Science Revision Guides - OCR Science: Phase 2 — 25

ANTIBODIES AND IMMUNISATION

Health In The Balance — 7

HIGHER TIER

1. After 2 weeks, in her first term of teaching, Miss Barton suffered a cold and a sore throat.

   a) Explain what caused Miss Barton to feel ill.

   b) All the other teachers said that when they started teaching they seemed to get ill more often. Can you explain this?

   c) Miss Barton recovered from her cold without taking any medicines. Explain how.

   d) After her first year of teaching Miss Barton became less prone to becoming ill. Explain why.

2. Doctors have recently become concerned at the rise in number of cases of tuberculosis. Tuberculosis had almost been wiped out as a disease due to the BCG vaccination which injects a person with a mild form of the bacterium. Explain how the BCG vaccination works.

3. Some diseases, such as measles, we get once and never again. Explain why this is so.

4. Tetanus is a bacterium. It releases a toxin which causes paralysis when in the body. Explain **TWO** ways in which the body will try to fight off infection from tetanus.

DRUGS

Health In The Balance — 8

1. The table shows the effect of smoking and the chances of getting cancer.

NUMBER OF CIGARETTES SMOKED PER DAY	INCREASED CHANCE OF LUNG CANCER COMPARED TO NON-SMOKERS
5	4x
10	8x
15	12x
20	16x

a) What effect does smoking cigarettes have on the chance of getting lung cancer?

b) Why does smoking affect the lungs, in particular?

c) Which substance in tobacco is addictive?

d) Name **THREE** other diseases caused by smoking.

(i)　　　　　(ii)　　　　　(iii)

e) What are the harmful effects of smoking on the circulatory system?

2. Alcohol is a legal drug.

a) What effect does moderate alcohol consumption have on the body?

b) Name **THREE** reasons why driving under the influence of alcohol is inadvisable.

c) State **TWO** long-term health problems associated with excess alcohol consumption.

(i)　　　　　(ii)

3. a) What are solvents?

b) State **THREE** problems caused by solvent abuse.

(i)　　　　　(ii)　　　　　(iii)

ALKANES AND ALKENES 1

Carbon Chemistry 1

1. What is a hydrocarbon?

2. a) Methane is an alkane. What do we mean by an alkane?

   b) Ethene is an alkene. Explain the meaning of the term 'alkene'.

   c) What is the difference between an alkane and an alkene?

   d) Describe how bromine water can be used to test for an alkene.

   e) Draw the displayed formulae for ethene, C_2H_4 and ethane C_2H_6, and label them accordingly.

3. a) Complete the following table.

NAME OF HYDROCARBON	PROPANE	
MOLECULAR FORMULA		C_3H_6
DISPLAYED FORMULA		

   b) Which hydrocarbon contains one double carbon carbon covalent bond? Explain your answer.

   c) Which hydrocarbon would decolourise bromine water? Explain your answer.

ALKANES AND ALKENES II

Carbon Chemistry 2 — HIGHER TIER

1. a) Alkanes are a series of saturated hydrocarbons. Explain this statement.

b) Complete the following table.

Name of alkane		PENTANE	
n			8
Molecular Formula		C_5H_{12}	
Displayed Formula	H—C—C—C—H (with H's)		

2. a) Alkenes are a series of unsaturated hydrocarbons. Explain this statement.

b) Complete the following table.

Name of alkene			
n			10
Molecular Formula		C_5H_{10}	
Displayed Formula	C=C—C—C—H (with H's)		

3. a) What is an addition reaction?

b) Complete the following by drawing the displayed formula of the product formed during the following addition reactions.

i) CH₂=CH—CH₂—H + H_2 →

ii) CH₂=CH—CH₂—H + $Br_{2(aq)}$ →

c) What conditions are necessary for the addition reaction in b) i)?

CRACKING

Carbon Chemistry 3

1. The bar chart shows the economic demand for the fractions of crude oil and the relative amounts of each fraction in crude oil.

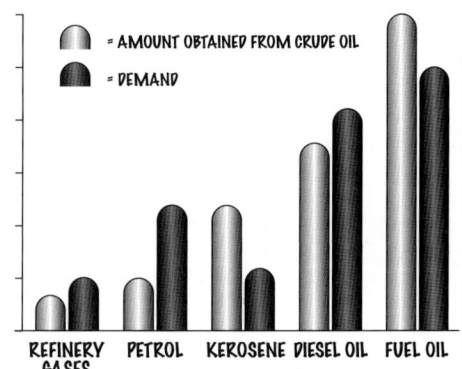

   a) Which fraction is in least demand?

   b) In which fraction is the amount obtained equal to twice the demand?

   c) Apart from petrol name TWO other fractions where demand exceeds supply.
   i) .... ii) ....

   d) Suggest a reason why the demand for petrol exceeds the supply of petrol.

   e) Explain how oil refineries match their output to the demand for different fractions.

2. The diagram shows the apparatus used in the laboratory for cracking long chain hydrocarbons.

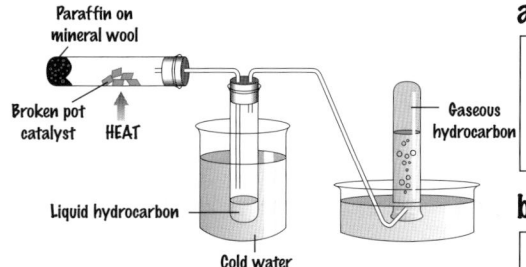

   a) What do we mean by 'cracking long chain hydrocarbons'?

   b) What is the purpose of the 'broken pot catalyst'?

   HIGHER TIER

   c) The alkane chosen for cracking has the chemical formula $C_{12}H_{26}$. The equation for the reaction is:

   $$C_{12}H_{26} \longrightarrow C_xH_y + C_2H_4$$

   Use the equation to work out the formula of C_xH_y.

   d) Which of the above products of the reaction is an unsaturated hydrocarbon? Explain your choice.

   e) Explain how it is possible to obtain a mixture of other products during the cracking of $C_{12}H_{26}$.

ADDITION POLYMERISATION

Carbon Chemistry — 4

1. a) What is a monomer?

   b) Many molecules of ethene can be joined together to form poly(ethene). What happens to each ethene molecule for this to happen?

   c) What is the name given to the reaction above?

   d) What conditions are necessary for the above reaction to take place?

   e) Complete the following equation to show how **FOUR** ethene molecules join together to form part of a poly(ethene) molecule.

$$\begin{array}{c}H\\H\end{array}C=C\begin{array}{c}H\\H\end{array} + \begin{array}{c}H\\H\end{array}C=C\begin{array}{c}H\\H\end{array} + \begin{array}{c}H\\H\end{array}C=C\begin{array}{c}H\\H\end{array} + \begin{array}{c}H\\H\end{array}C=C\begin{array}{c}H\\H\end{array} \longrightarrow$$

2. a) Propene is another alkene which can form a long chain molecule (polymer). What is the name given to the polymer?

   b) Complete the following equation to show how **FOUR** propene molecules join together to form part of its polymer.

$$\begin{array}{c}H\\H\end{array}C=C\begin{array}{c}CH_3\\H\end{array} + \begin{array}{c}H\\H\end{array}C=C\begin{array}{c}CH_3\\H\end{array} + \begin{array}{c}H\\H\end{array}C=C\begin{array}{c}CH_3\\H\end{array} + \begin{array}{c}H\\H\end{array}C=C\begin{array}{c}CH_3\\H\end{array} \longrightarrow$$

   c) Name **TWO** other addition polymers and the monomers from which they are made.

   i)

   ii)

---- HIGHER TIER ----

3. The diagram below shows part of a polymer

$$-\underset{H}{\overset{H}{C}}-\underset{Cl}{\overset{H}{C}}-\underset{H}{\overset{H}{C}}-\underset{Cl}{\overset{H}{C}}-\underset{H}{\overset{H}{C}}-\underset{Cl}{\overset{H}{C}}-\underset{H}{\overset{H}{C}}-\underset{Cl}{\overset{H}{C}}-$$

Which one of the following monomers is it made from, C_3H_5Cl or C_2H_3Cl? Explain your choice.

PLASTICS

Carbon Chemistry — 5

1. State a suitable polymer for the following applications.

   (i) Fast food packaging ....
   (ii) Making wooden toys ....
   (iii) Insulation ....
   (iv) Take-away coffee cups ....
   (v) Carrier Bags ....

2. a) As a nation, we produce a large amount of plastic waste. Explain why.

   ....

   b) List three ways in which plastics can be disposed of.

   (i) ....
   (ii) ....
   (iii) ....

   c) Describe a disadvantage of each of the above methods of disposal.

   (i) ....
   (ii) ....
   (iii) ....

   d) State which method you would use. Discuss your answer.

   ....

---- HIGHER TIER ----

3. a) Some plastics can be easily stretched while others are rigid. Explain, in terms of their structure, why this is.

   ....

   b) Plastics that can be easily stretched have high melting points. True or False? Explain your answer.

   ....

COVALENT BONDING

Carbon Chemistry — 6

1. a) What is a molecule?

   b) A molecule of water is made up of 1 atom of oxygen and 2 atoms of hydrogen. The diagram opposite shows the electron arrangements for hydrogen and oxygen. Explain, using a diagram, how these atoms form a water molecule.

   c) A molecule of carbon dioxide is made up of 1 atom of carbon and 2 atoms of oxygen. The diagram opposite shows the electron arrangements for carbon and oxygen. Explain, using a diagram, how these atoms form a carbon dioxide molecule.

   d) Name one property common to both water and carbon dioxide.

---- HIGHER TIER ----

2. Complete the following table. This first one is done for you.

MOLECULE	FORMULA	DISPLAYED FORMULA	DOT AND CROSS MODEL
HYDROGEN	H_2	H – H	H H
CHLORINE			
		H–C–H (with H above and below)	
	C_2H_4		

3. a) Explain why simple covalently bonded molecules have low melting and boiling points.

   b) They also have another common characteristic. State what it is and give a reason for it.

CARBON

Carbon Chemistry — 7

1. a) Connect the words DIAMOND and GRAPHITE to the correct statement.

   DIAMOND

   - Has a very high melting point
   - Is soft
   - Does not conduct electricity
   - Carbon atoms are bonded to each other
   - Is very hard
   - Does conduct electricity

   GRAPHITE

   b) What is the name of the third form of carbon? ....

HIGHER TIER

2. The diagrams show two structures of carbon.

   a) State which structure is graphite and which structure is diamond.

   A: .... B: ....

   b) What is the difference between the two structures?

   ....
   ....
   ....

   c) Explain the following:

   (i) Diamond has a very high melting point.

   ....

   (ii) Graphite conducts electricity but diamond does not.

   ....

   (iii) Graphite can be used as a lubricant.

   ....

FORMULAE AND EQUATIONS

Chemical Economics 1

1. Complete the table below by writing down which elements are found in the compound and how many atoms there are in one molecule of the compound. One has been done for you.

	ELEMENTS	ATOMS
a) Methane, CH_4	CARBON, HYDROGEN	5
b) Hydrochloric Acid, HCl		
c) Nitric Acid, HNO_3		
d) Octane, C_8H_{18}		
e) Water, H_2O		
f) Aluminium Chloride, $AlCl_3$		
g) Calcium Hydroxide, $Ca(OH)_2$		
h) Magnesium Nitrate, $Mg(NO_3)_2$		
i) Aluminium Sulphate, $Al_2(SO_4)_3$		

2. In each of the following word equations, write 'reactant' or 'product' under each substance to show which they are.

a) iron + sulphur ⟶ iron sulphide

b) calcium + water ⟶ calcium hydroxide + hydrogen

3. Below are a number of symbol equations. Convert each one into a word equation.

a) Complete each symbol equation by adding state symbols.
b) Convert each symbol equation into a word equation.

i) $2H_2\ (\ \ )$ + $O_2\ (\ \ )$ ⟶ $2H_2O\ (\ \ )$

ii) $2Na\ (\ \ )$ + $2H_2O\ (\ \ )$ ⟶ $2NaOH\ (\ \ )$ + $H_2\ (\ \ )$

iii) $2Mg\ (\ \ )$ + $O_2\ (\ \ )$ ⟶ $2MgO\ (\ \ )$

WRITING BALANCED SYMBOL EQUATIONS

Chemical Economics — 2

1. For each of the following chemical reactions ...
   - Draw atoms/molecules under each equation IN THE CORRECT NUMBERS to illustrate what is taking place.
   - Write the names of all substances underneath them.

eg. $2Na_{(s)} + 2H_2O_{(l)} \rightarrow 2NaOH_{(aq)} + H_{2(g)}$

Sodium + Water → Sodium Hydroxide + Hydrogen

a) $2Fe_{(s)} + 3Cl_{2(g)} \rightarrow 2FeCl_{3(s)}$

b) $Mg_{(s)} + 2H_2O_{(l)} \rightarrow Mg(OH)_{2(aq)} + H_{2(g)}$

2. Here are some chemical reactions shown first as a word equation and then as a symbol equation. Balance the symbol equations.

a) calcium + oxygen → calcium oxide
   ___$Ca_{(s)}$ + ___$O_{2(g)}$ → ___$CaO_{(s)}$

b) zinc + hydrochloric acid → zinc chloride + hydrogen
   ___$Zn_{(s)}$ + ___$HCl_{(aq)}$ → ___$ZnCl_{2(aq)}$ + ___$H_{2(g)}$

c) sodium hydroxide + sulphuric acid → sodium sulphate + water
   ___$NaOH_{(aq)}$ + ___$H_2SO_{4(aq)}$ → ___$Na_2SO_{4(aq)}$ + ___$H_2O_{(l)}$

d) magnesium + sulphuric acid → magnesium sulphate + hydrogen
   ___$Mg_{(s)}$ + ___$H_2SO_{4(aq)}$ → ___$MgSO_{4(aq)}$ + ___$H_{2(g)}$

HIGHER TIER

e) aluminium + sulphuric acid → aluminium sulphate + hydrogen
   ___$Al_{(s)}$ + ___$H_2SO_{4(aq)}$ → ___$Al_2(SO_4)_{3(aq)}$ + ___$H_{2(g)}$

RELATIVE FORMULA MASS

Chemical Economics — 3

1. Use a data book or a periodic table to find out the relative atomic mass of the following elements:

a) Beryllium	j) Francium
b) Aluminium	k) Nitrogen
c) Chlorine	l) Boron
d) Titanium	m) Helium
e) Bromine	n) Krypton
f) Argon	o) Molybdenum
g) Tellurium	p) Niobium
h) Lithium	q) Calcium
i) Tungsten	r) Germanium

2. Calculate the relative formula mass of the following compounds (a periodic table or your data book will be useful).

a) Water, H_2O	g) Aluminium Chloride, $AlCl_3$
b) Sodium Chloride, $NaCl$	h) Sulphuric Acid, H_2SO_4
c) Copper Oxide, CuO	i) Ethene, C_2H_4
d) Aluminium Oxide, Al_2O_3	j) Sodium Carbonate, Na_2CO_3
e) Copper Sulphate, $CuSO_4$	k) Aluminium Sulphate, $Al_2(SO_4)_3$
f) Calcium Hydroxide, $Ca(OH)_2$	l) Ammonia, NH_3

3. For each of the following compounds 'X' is an unknown element. The relative formula mass of the compound is given in the bracket. Work out which element X represents.

a) XO (40)	e) X_2O (62)
b) XCl_2 (110)	f) MgX_2 (94)
c) CX_2 (44)	g) $X(OH)_2$ (171)
d) XNO_3 (63)	h) X_2O_3 (188)

OCR Reference: Page 44

CALCULATING MASSES OF PRODUCTS AND REACTANTS
Chemical Economics — 4

HIGHER TIER

1. Calcium carbonate and hydrochloric acid react together to produce calcium chloride, carbon dioxide and water. Below is the balanced symbol equation for this reaction. Use this in the following questions.

   a) Work out the M_r for each of the reactants and products shown in the equation and write them in the boxes.

   $CaCO_{3(s)}$ + $2HCl_{(aq)}$ → $CaCl_{2(aq)}$ + $CO_{2(g)}$ + $H_2O_{(l)}$

   [ ] + [ ] → [ ] + [ ] + [ ]

   b) What is the total mass of the substances on the left-hand side of the equation? [ ]

   c) What is the total mass of the substances on the right-hand side of the equation? [ ]

   d) Would you have expected the masses in part b) and c) to be the same?

   e) What mass of calcium chloride can be produced from 2 grams of calcium carbonate?

   f) A tonne of calcium carbonate would produce what mass of water if it was fully reacted with hydrochloric acid?

   g) What mass of hydrochloric acid would be needed to fully react with 25 grams of calcium carbonate?

EMPIRICAL FORMULAE

Chemical Economics 5

HIGHER TIER

- Use the following relative atomic masses (A_r) to help you work out the empirical formula of each of the following compounds.

  Relative atomic masses: Na = 23, Cu = 64, C = 12, O = 16, Ca = 40, S = 32

1. Find the simplest formula of the compound formed when 1.15g of sodium combines with 0.40g of oxygen.

2. 2g of copper reacted with 0.25g of oxygen to form an oxide of copper. Work out its simplest formula.

3. A compound consists of 40% calcium, 12% carbon, and 48% oxygen. Deduce its empirical formula.

4. If 0.1g of sulphur burns to form 0.2g of sulphur dioxide, work out the empirical formula of the oxide produced.

OCR Reference: Page 46

THE MOLE AND MOLAR MASS

Chemical Economics — 6

You will need a data book or periodic table to be able to do the calculations on this page. Show your working.

HIGHER TIER

1. Calculate the molar mass of the following:

a) Magnesium, Mg

b) Magnesium Chloride, $MgCl_2$

c) Water, H_2O

d) Aluminium Oxide, Al_2O_3

e) Sulphuric Acid, H_2SO_4

f) Ammonium Nitrate, NH_4NO_3

2. Calculate the number of moles in the following:

a) 24g of Carbon

b) 330g of Calcium Chloride, $CaCl_2$

c) 50g of Calcium Carbonate, $CaCO_3$

d) 4.25g of Ammonia, NH_3

e) 24.5g of Sulphuric Acid, H_2SO_4

f) 126g of Nitric Acid, HNO_3

3. Calculate the mass of the following:

a) 3 moles of Carbon Dioxide, CO_2

b) 15 moles of Sulphuric Acid, H_2SO_4

c) 0.75 moles of Hydrochloric Acid, HCl

d) 0.01 moles of Nitric Acid, HNO_3

4. For each of the following compounds 'X' is an unknown element. The molar mass of the compound is given in the bracket. Work out which element X represents.

a) XO (40g/mol)

b) XO_2 (56g/mol)

c) $X(OH)_2$ (74g/mol)

d) X_2CO_3 (106g/mol)

PERCENTAGE YIELD

1. Complete the following table. The first one is done for you.

Actual Yield	Predicted Yield	Percentage Yield
12g	20g	$\frac{12g}{20g} \times 100\% = 60\%$
6g	8g	
1.2g	1.8g	
44kg	44kg	
0.8g	6.4g	
	25kg	50%
63g		90%

2. An experiment was carried out to produce the salt copper sulphate, details of which are given below. The actual yield of copper sulphate was 4.2g while the predicted yield was 5g.

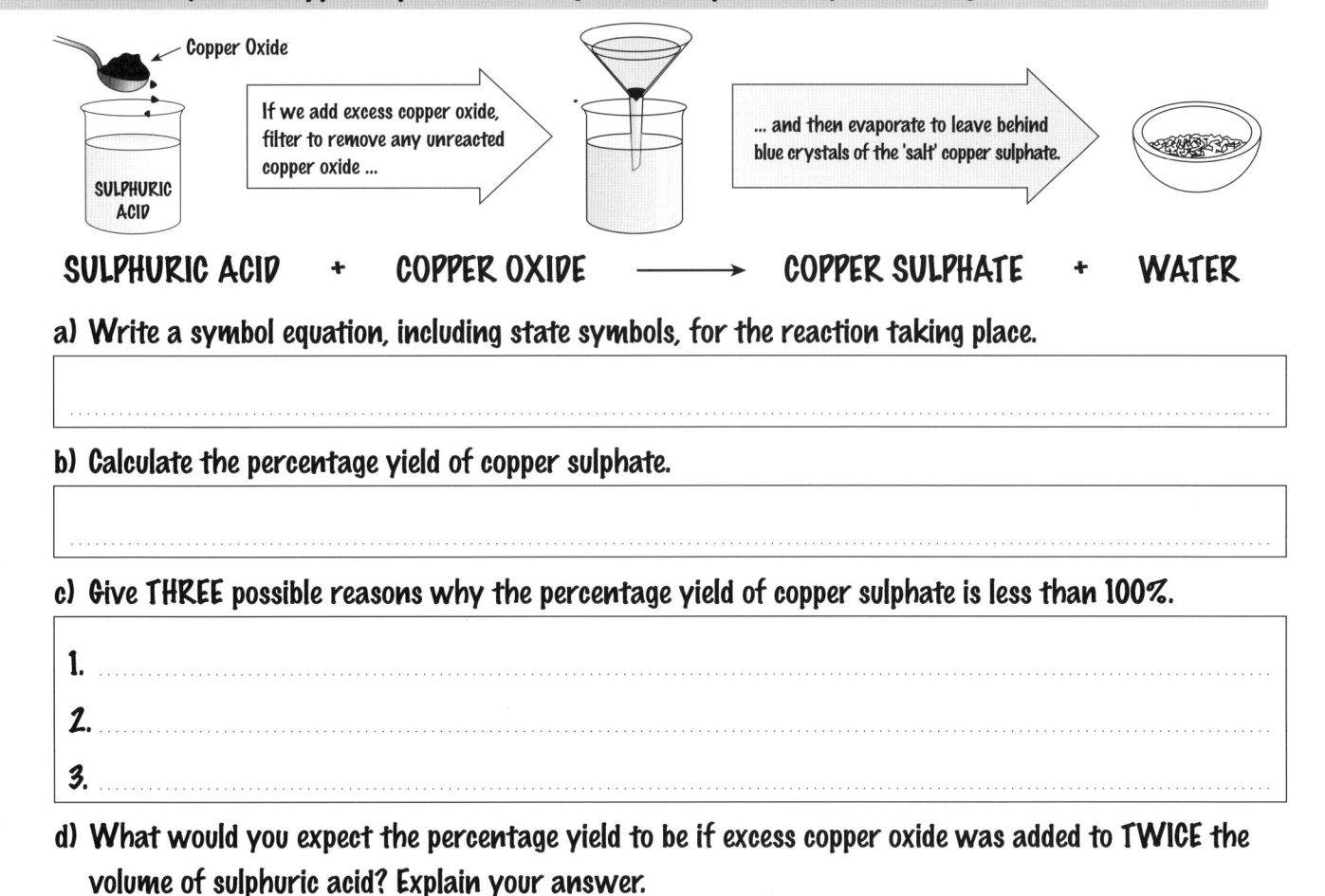

SULPHURIC ACID + COPPER OXIDE ⟶ COPPER SULPHATE + WATER

If we add excess copper oxide, filter to remove any unreacted copper oxide ... and then evaporate to leave behind blue crystals of the 'salt' copper sulphate.

a) Write a symbol equation, including state symbols, for the reaction taking place.

b) Calculate the percentage yield of copper sulphate.

c) Give THREE possible reasons why the percentage yield of copper sulphate is less than 100%.

1.
2.
3.

d) What would you expect the percentage yield to be if excess copper oxide was added to TWICE the volume of sulphuric acid? Explain your answer.

PRODUCTION OF AMMONIA

Chemical Economics — 8

1. a) The Haber process is used to make Ammonia. Complete the diagram of the process by filling in the spaces.

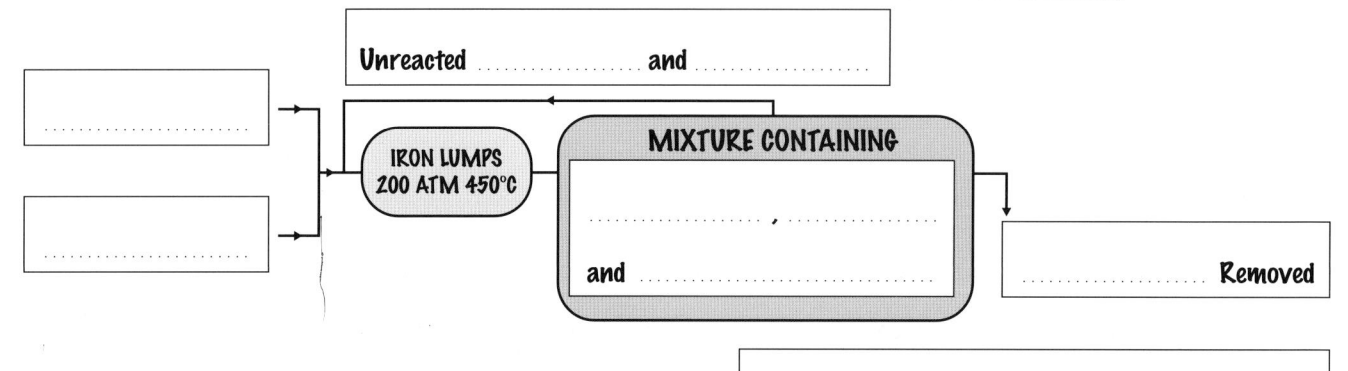

   Unreacted .... and ....

   [............] → [IRON LUMPS 200 ATM 450°C] → MIXTURE CONTAINING .... , ... and .... → .... Removed

   [............]

   b) Where is the raw material nitrogen obtained from?

   c) Explain why the nitrogen and hydrogen is passed over iron.

   d) How is the ammonia separated from the other gases at the end of the process?

   e) What would happen to a piece of damp universal indicator paper if it was held in some ammonia gas?

   f) The production of ammonia is an example of a reversible reaction. Explain what this means.

   g) What effect does high pressure have on the reaction?

   h) Why is a temperature of 450°C chosen when producing ammonia?

2. Below is a graph typical of the percentage yield of ammonia at different temperatures and pressures.

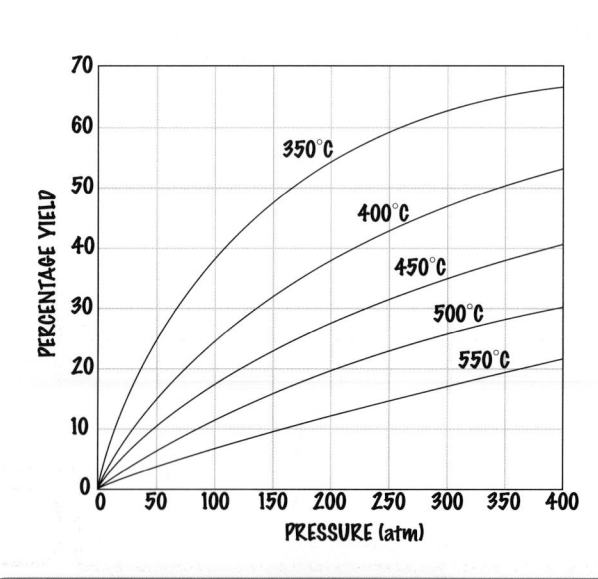

   a) Why is a temperature of 550°C and pressure of 400atm not chosen for the reaction?

   b) The higher the pressure, the greater the percentage yield. Why is too high a pressure not used?

ECONOMICS OF MAKING SUBSTANCES

Chemical Economics — 9

1. Name FIVE things which the cost of making a new substance would depend on.

   i) ....
   ii) ....
   iii) ....
   iv) ....
   v) ....

2. In what way do the following factors affect the cost of making a new substance?

   i) Pressure: ....
   ii) Temperature: ....
   iii) Use of catalyst: ....
   iv) Recycling: ....
   v) Automation: ....

---- HIGHER TIER ----

3. a) Why is a low percentage yield acceptable in the manufacture of a substance?

   b) Is cost or yield more important in the manufacture of a substance? Explain your answer.

4. a) Why does a low temperature favour the production of ammonia?

   b) A high temperature would make ammonia form faster.
      What disadvantage is there in using a high temperature?

   c) Why does high pressure favour the production of ammonia?

   d) What effect does the use of a catalyst have on ...
      i) rate of reaction?
      ii) percentage yield?

OCR Reference: Page 50 — Lonsdale Science Revision Guides - OCR Science: Phase 2

ACIDS, BASES AND NEUTRALISATION

1. a) What is an acid?

b) What is a base?

2. A beaker containing 100cm³ of sodium hydroxide has universal indicator solution added to it. Sulphuric acid was then added using a burette and the pH of the solution was estimated by gauging the colour of the liquid. The solution was constantly stirred. The results are shown below.

VOLUME OF ACID ADDED (cm³)	0	4	12	30	50
pH OF SOLUTION	14	12	10	8	7

a) Plot a graph of these results.

b) What colour was the solution at the start?

c) What colour was the solution at the end?

d) Write a symbol equation for the reaction taking place.

e) What is the name given to this type of reaction?

HIGHER TIER

3. a) The reaction of an acid with an alkali gives us a salt and water. Complete the following word equations:

(i) Sodium Hydroxide + Hydrochloric Acid ⟶ .... + Water

(ii) .... + Nitric Acid ⟶ Calcium Nitrate + Water

(iii) Potassium Hydroxide + Nitric Acid ⟶ .... + Water

(iv) Calcium Hydroxide + ... ⟶ Calcium Chloride + Water

(v) Potassium Hydroxide + ... ⟶ Potassium Chloride + Water

(vi) Ammonia + Sulphuric Acid ⟶

b) Write balanced symbol equations, including state symbols for the six reactions in part a).

i)   iv)

ii)   v)

iii) vi)

FERTILISERS AND EUTROPHICATION — Chemical Economics — 11

1. a) Name FOUR different fertilisers.

   i) .... ii) .... iii) .... iv) ....

   b) i) Which fertiliser is made by neutralising sulphuric acid with ammonia?

   ....

   ii) Which fertiliser is made by neutralising nitric acid with ammonia?

   ....

   c) Name the THREE main elements found in fertilisers.

   i) .... ii) .... iii) ....

   d) Why do farmers use fertilisers?

   ....

   e) Why must fertilisers be soluble in water?

   ....

   f) What economic advantage is there for a farmer to use fertiliser?

   ....

   HIGHER TIER

   g) Why is it important that fertilisers provide nitrogen in the form of soluble nitrates?

   ....

2. The diagram shows an arable farm (growing wheat, for example). The farm is intensively farmed and the farmer uses a lot of fertiliser to increase his yields.

   Water from the farm drains into the stream labelled A. This then drains into the River Lonsdale at B. The river has an abundance of fish at X. Anglers are increasingly complaining about the lack of fish at Z.

   a) Explain why there is a lot of growth of simple algae at Y.

   ....

   b) Explain how this growth of simple algae can eventually affect the population of fish in the river.

   ....

OCR Reference: Page 52 — *Lonsdale* Science Revision Guides - OCR Science: Phase 2

ATOMS I

The Periodic Table 1

1. a) Complete the table about atomic particles.

Atomic Particle	Relative Mass	Relative Charge
		+1
	1	
	0.0005	

b) Describe the structure of the atom in terms of these particles.

2. Complete the following table. You may need to refer to a data book or Periodic Table of the elements. The first one is done for you.

Element name	Symbol	Mass Number	Atomic Number
Sodium	Na	23	11
Magnesium			
Aluminium			
	C		
	N		
		16	
			7

3. Explain why ...

a) only the masses of the protons and neutrons in an atom contribute significantly to its mass.

b) an atom has no overall (net) electrical charge.

4. a) What do we mean by the term ISOTOPE?

The following show symbol representations of two isotopes of hydrogen.

b) How do we know that they are isotopes of HYDROGEN?

(i) $^{1}_{1}H$

(ii) $^{2}_{1}H$

ATOMS II

The Periodic Table — HIGHER TIER

1. In the nucleus of a potassium atom there are 19 protons and 20 neutrons.

    a) What is the mass number of potassium?

    b) What is the atomic number of potassium?

    c) How many electrons does a neutral atom of potassium contain?

    d) Why is an atom of potassium neutral?

2. a) The letters A, B, C, D, E, F and G below represent seven different elements.

    For each one write down (i) their atomic number (ii) their mass number (iii) the number of protons and (iv) the number of neutrons in one atom (A, B, C, D, E, F, G are not their chemical symbols).

	$^{12}_{6}A$	$^{9}_{4}B$	$^{19}_{9}C$	$^{11}_{5}D$	$^{28}_{14}E$	$^{40}_{18}F$	$^{35}_{17}G$
(i) Atomic No.							
(ii) Mass No.							
(iii) No. of Protons							
(iv) No. of Neutrons							

   b) Use a periodic table to identify the elements, A, B, C, D, E, F and G.

   A=   B=   C=   D=

   E=   F=   G=

   c) Explain what is meant by: (i) Atomic number:

   (ii) Mass number:

3. Complete the following table. The first one has been done for you.

	$^{14}_{7}N$	$^{197}_{79}Au$	$^{235}_{92}U$	Ca	$^{84}_{36}$	226		Fe
No. of Protons	7			20				26
No. of Neutrons	7			20			34	30
No. of Electrons	7					88		
Element	Nitrogen				Krypton			

4. a) What is the difference between a potassium (K) atom and a potassium (K^+) ion?

   b) What is the difference between a sulphur (S) atom and a sulphide (S^{2-}) ion?

OCR Reference: Page 55   Lonsdale Science Revision Guides - OCR Science: Phase 2

THE PERIODIC TABLE

1. The diagram shows an outline of the periodic table.

a) Colour in the area where you would find the metal elements.

b) Write down the name of the following elements whose symbols are given below and then put the symbols of these elements on the periodic table. (Use your revision guide to help you.)

(i) Li:	(ii) Fe:	(iii) Zn:	(iv) Au:
(v) Na:	(vi) Cu:	(vii) Pb:	(viii) Ca:
(ix) Mg:	(x) H:	(xi) B:	(xii) Al:
(xiii) Ar:	(xiv) Cl:	(xv) He:	(xvi) F:

2. Using only the elements above, answer the following questions:

a) Write the name and symbol of:

i) a metal ....

(ii) a non-metal ....

iii) Two metals in the same group: ....

iv) Two non-metals in the same group: ....

v) Two elements that have 1 electron in their outer shell: ....

vi) Two elements that have 8 electrons in their outer shell: ....

vii) Two elements that are in the same period: ....

b) Name ONE metal that has similar properties to magnesium. Explain your choice.

3. The following wordsearch contains **TEN** metals. Write down each one with its symbol.

(i) ....
(ii) ....
(iii) ....
(iv) ....
(v) ....
(vi) ....
(vii) ....
(viii) ....
(ix) ....
(x) ....

```
S A I P H C S A G F I R O C U L
L I T H I U M S H P U O J M K I
B W R O U P A L U M I N I U M T
P L I U M P G B T R V G B I A H
A I S Q U E N S Z P O T O K G P
T G O L D T E S I R O N R A N C
V O D B A I S Y N G B H G E I A
P D I U M U I D C O P P E R J L
P S U B S S U O B L G A L L W C
E F M O I U M A G H O I U B A I
R A L R F G T D N R X W T D P U
M B T Y V A G P O T A S S I U M
```

4. Why are potassium and chlorine both elements while potassium chloride is a compound?

ELECTRONIC STRUCTURE OF THE FIRST TWENTY ELEMENTS

The Periodic Table — 4

HIGHER TIER

1. In the spaces provided draw electron configuration diagrams for the following elements.

$_1$H	$_4$Be	$_{20}$Ca	$_{14}$Si	$_{16}$S
$_6$C	$_{18}$Ar	$_{11}$Na	$_{19}$K	$_{13}$Al

2. Complete the following. The first one has been done for you.

Lithium, Li
Proton No. = 3
No. of electrons = 3
Electron config. = 2, 1
Electron config. diagram

Aluminium, Al
Proton No. = 13
No. of electrons = 13
Electron config. = 2, 8, 3
Electron config. diagram

_____ , _____
Proton No. =
No. of electrons =
Electron config. = 2, 5
Electron config. diagram

_____ , _____
Proton No. = 2
No. of electrons =
Electron config. =
Electron config. diagram

Chlorine, _____
Proton No. =
No. of electrons =
Electron config. =
Electron config. diagram

_____ , _____
Proton No. =
No. of electrons =
Electron config. =
Electron config. diagram

_____ , _____
Proton No. =
No. of electrons =
Electron config. = 2, 3
Electron config. diagram

_____ , Ne
Proton No. =
No. of electrons =
Electron config. =
Electron config. diagram

3. Below are the electron configurations for eight elements. To which period does each element belong to?

ELECTRON CONFIGURATION	PERIOD	ELECTRON CONFIGURATION	PERIOD
(i) 2, 7		(v) 2, 8, 6	
(ii) 2, 8, 8		(vi) 2, 8, 8, 1	
(iii) 2, 4		(vii) 2, 2	
(iv) 2, 8, 2		(viii) 2, 8, 5	

OCR Reference: Page 57

THE ELEMENTS OF GROUP 1

The Periodic Table — 5

1. Lithium is the first element of Group 1 of the periodic table. A piece of lithium is placed onto some water. The water has universal indicator in it.

   a) Why does the lithium float?

   b) What happens to the lithium?

   c) The colour of the water turns from green to purple. Explain why.

   d) Name the next two elements of Group 1 of the periodic table.

   (i)   (ii)

   e) Describe how each of these elements would react with water (compare your answer to the description you gave for lithium above).

   (i)

   (ii)

   f) i) Write a word equation for the reaction taking place between lithium and water.

   ═══ HIGHER TIER ═══

   ii) Write a symbol equation for the reaction taking place between lithium and water.

   g) Why would you not carry out the reaction between rubidium and water?

2. The graph below shows the density of the first five elements of group 1. They are not in order.

   a) Name the five elements A to E.

   A: B:
   C: D:
   E:

   b) What trend is there in the density of the alkali metals as we go down the group?

THE ELEMENTS OF GROUP 7

The Periodic Table — 6

1. Fluorine and chlorine are both elements found in group 7 of the periodic table.

   a) Why do fluorine and chlorine have similar properties?

   b) Write down a word equation for the reaction of fluorine gas with sodium.

   HIGHER TIER

   c) Write a balanced symbol equation for the above reaction.

2. Ronny carried out an experiment to see how halogens (Group 7) react with other halogen compounds. He added aqueous solutions of bromine, iodine and chlorine, in turn, to aqueous solutions of sodium chloride, sodium bromide and sodium iodide.

   a) Complete the table of results below where ✓ = reaction and ✗ = no reaction

	Sodium Iodide (NaI)	Sodium Chloride (NaCl)	Sodium Bromide (NaBr)
Bromine			
Iodine			
Chlorine			

   b) Why was the experiment carried out in a fume cupboard?

   c) Write a word equation for any of the above reactions.

   HIGHER TIER

3. The following table shows the boiling point of the first five elements of group 7. They are not in order.

ELEMENT	BOILING POINTS
A	59°C
B	337°C
C	-188°C
D	184°C
E	-34°C

   a) Name the five elements A to E.

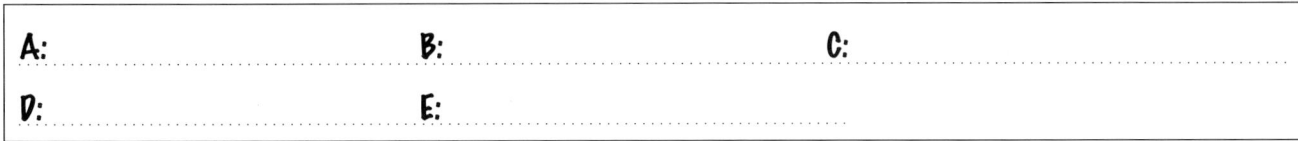

   A: B: C:

   D: E:

   b) Draw a bar graph to show the data in the table.

   c) What trend is there in the boiling point of the halogens as we go down the group?

TRENDS IN REACTIVITY WITHIN GROUPS 1 AND 7

The Periodic Table — 7

HIGHER TIER

1. a) Explain why alkali metals have similar properties when they react.

   b) In terms of the transfer of electrons, what is an oxidation reaction?

   c) Put dots or crosses onto the rings in the boxes to show the electron configurations of the atoms and ions of the two alkali metals, sodium and potassium. A sodium atom has 11 electrons and a potassium ion has 18 electrons.

   i) SODIUM ATOM   SODIUM ION

   ii) POTASSIUM ATOM   POTASSIUM ION

   d) Why do the alkali metals become more reactive as we go down the group?

2. a) Explain why the halogens have similar properties when they react.

   b) In terms of the transfer of electrons, what is a reduction reaction?

   c) Put dots or crosses onto the rings in the boxes to show the electron configurations of the atoms and ions of the two halogens, fluorine and chlorine.
   A fluorine atom has 9 electrons and a chloride ion has 18 electrons.

   i) FLUORINE ATOM   FLUORIDE ION

   ii) CHLORINE ATOM   CHLORIDE ION

   d) Why do the halogens become less reactive as we go down the group?

THE ELEMENTS OF GROUP 8

The Periodic Table — 8

1. The table below shows information about the elements known as the noble gases, Group 8.

Noble Gas	Atomic Number	Melting Point (°C)	Boiling Point (°C)
	2	-272	-269
Neon		-248	-246
	18	-189	-189
Krypton	36	-157	-153

   a) Complete the first two columns of the table.

   b) Describe the change in melting point and boiling point as you go down the group.

   c) How does the density of the noble gases change as we go up the group?

   d) All of these gases are monatomic. What do we mean by monatomic?

   e) Explain why ...

   (i) helium is used in airships

   (ii) argon is used in light bulbs

   (iii) neon is used in discharge tubes

---- HIGHER TIER ----

2. a) Draw electron configuration diagrams for an atom of neon and argon.

   NEON

   ARGON

   b) By reference to the diagrams in part 2a), explain why the noble gases are so UNREACTIVE.

   c) The noble gases were not discovered until 1898. Explain why.

   d) Before they were called the noble gases, these elements were at one time called the inert gases. Explain why.

BONDING OF IONS

The Periodic Table — 9

1. a) What is an ion?

   b) Explain how a positive ion is formed.

   c) Explain how a negative ion is formed.

2. The diagram below shows the structure of sodium chloride. Explain how sodium and chlorine atoms combine to form this structure.

   Na^+ ion Cl^- ion

3. Connect the compounds sodium chloride and magnesium oxide to the correct statements.

   - Dissolves in water
   - Conducts electricity when molten
   - Has a very high melting point
   - Does not conduct electricity when solid
   - Conducts electricity when it is in solution

   SODIUM CHLORIDE   MAGNESIUM OXIDE

HIGHER TIER

4. Explain why ...

   a) Sodium chloride has a high melting point.

   b) Magnesium oxide conducts electricity when molten.

   c) Sodium chloride does not conduct electricity when solid.

---

54 — Lonsdale Science Revision Guides - OCR Science: Phase 2 — OCR Reference: Page 62

IONIC BONDING

The Periodic Table — 10

HIGHER TIER

1. Magnesium and chlorine react together to produce magnesium chloride. The equation for this reaction is ... Mg + Cl$_2$ → MgCl$_2$

   a) Use a periodic table to find the atomic numbers of magnesium and chlorine.

   MAGNESIUM = ... CHLORINE = ...

   b) Draw electron configuration diagrams for a magnesium atom and a chlorine atom.

   MAGNESIUM   CHLORINE

   c) Magnesium chloride is an ionic compound. Explain how:

   (i) A magnesium atom becomes a magnesium ion.

   (ii) A chlorine atom becomes a chloride ion.

   d) Draw an electron configuration diagram of magnesium chloride, MgCl$_2$.

   e) Magnesium also reacts with oxygen to form magnesium oxide, MgO.

   (i) Explain how an oxygen atom becomes an oxide ion.

   (ii) Draw electron configuration diagrams for an oxygen atom and an oxide ion.

   OXYGEN ATOM   OXIDE ION

   f) Explain how the ionic bond is formed between magnesium and oxygen to produce magnesium oxide.

2. For each of the following compounds, three choices of formulae are given. Only one is correct. Underline the correct one.

   a) Calcium hydroxide: CaOH   Ca$_2$OH   Ca(OH)$_2$
   b) Magnesium oxide: MgO   Mg$_2$O   MgO$_2$
   c) Aluminium oxide: AlO   Al$_3$O$_2$ Al$_2$O$_3$
   d) Copper(II) chloride: CuCl   Cu$_2$Cl   CuCl$_2$
   e) Iron(II) sulphate: FeSO$_4$ Fe$_2$SO$_4$ Fe(SO$_4$)$_2$
   f) Iron(III) sulphate: Fe$_2$SO$_4$ Fe$_2$(SO$_4$)$_3$ Fe(SO$_4$)$_2$

THE TRANSITION METALS

The Periodic Table — 11

1. a) Give the names of five transition metals.

   1. _____   2. _____   3. _____   4. _____   5. _____

   b) List four properties that these metals have in common.

   1. _____   2. _____

   3. _____   4. _____

   c) Transition metals have many uses. For each of the uses listed below give a reason why the transition metal is used.

   (i) Iron for car bodies _____

   (ii) Copper for wiring _____

2. a) What is thermal decomposition?

   _____

   An experiment was carried out where different masses of copper carbonate were heated until they turned from a bluish green colour to a black colour. The results are shown in the table.

MASS BEFORE HEATING	MASS AFTER HEATING
0.75	0.5
1.25	0.8
0.5	0.3
1.0	0.65
0.25	0.16

   b) On the axes opposite draw a graph to show the results.

   c) Why does the mass decrease during the experiment?

   _____

   d) Write a word equation for the reaction taking place.

   _____

   e) Apart from a change in colour which other simple test could be carried out to show that a thermal decomposition reaction has taken place?

   _____

3. a) Describe simply how you would identify whether a compound in solution contains COPPER(II) ions.

   _____

   HIGHER TIER

   b) Write an ionic symbol equation for the precipitate formed.

   _____

SIMPLE CIRCUITS

Using Electricity — 1

1. a) Below are **FIVE** simple circuits (all the cells and lamps are identical).

   A   B   C   D   E

   (i)   Which circuit has the greatest potential difference? ....
   (ii) Which circuit has the least potential difference? ....
   (iii) Which circuit has the greatest resistance? ....
   (iv) Which circuit has the least resistance? ....

   b) Which circuit would have the brightest lamps?   Circuit: ....
   Explain your answer: ....

   c) Which circuit would have the dimmest lamps?   Circuit: ....
   Explain your answer: ....

   d) Which **TWO** circuits would have the same current flowing through them?

   Circuits: ...... and ......   Explain your answer: ....

   e) Draw a circuit diagram for Circuit B above.
      Include on your diagram:
      (i)   an open switch
      (ii) an ammeter to measure the current.
      (iii) a voltmeter to measure the total pd across the cells.

   f) What is the difference between a direct current and an alternating current?

   ....

   g) For the following electrical symbols write down the name of the component they represent.
      (i) [switch symbol]   (ii) [cell symbol]   (iii) [resistor symbol]   (iv) [ammeter symbol]

   h) Draw the symbols for these electrical components.
      (i) Battery   (ii) Variable Resistor   (iii) Voltmeter   (iv) Switch (closed)

OCR Reference: Page 66   *Lonsdale* Science Revision Guides - OCR Science: Phase 2   57

POWER AND ENERGY TRANSFER IN CIRCUITS

Using Electricity 2

1. a) Calculate the power rating of the following appliances.

APPLIANCE	WORKING CURRENT	VOLTAGE	POWER RATING (W)
Iron	4A	230V	
Kettle	10A	230V	
Hi-Fi	0.5A	230V	
Hoover	6A	230V	
Toaster	3A	230V	

b) How many joules of electrical energy does the toaster above transfer every second when it is switched on? Explain your answer.

2. An electric motor works at a current of 3A and a voltage of 24V. What is the power rating of the motor? (Remember formula, working and unit!)

---HIGHER TIER---

3. a) Complete the following table.

APPLIANCE	WORKING CURRENT	VOLTAGE	POWER RATING
Television		230V	200W
Cooker		230V	3000W
Hairdryer	4.5A		1035W
Electric Fire	8.7A		2000W

b) How is it possible for two different appliances to have the same power rating but different working currents?

ELECTRIC CHARGE

Using Electricity 3

HIGHER TIER

1. The diagram shows an electrical circuit.

   a) What do we mean by the term current?

   b) What actually flows around this circuit?

2. a) The circuit above is switched on for 60 seconds. The ammeter reading is 3A. Calculate the charge that flows in this time.

   b) If the circuit is switched on for 30 seconds and a charge of 450 coulombs flows calculate the current.

3. A current of 5A flows in a circuit. A total charge of 2000 coulombs passes a point in the circuit. Calculate how long the circuit has been switched on for.

4. In the circuit shown, the reading on the ammeter is 3A. If the lamp is switched on for 5 minutes calculate the charge that flows. (Remember formula, working and unit!)

5. a) During the electrolysis of Copper (II) Chloride the ammeter reading was 6A. If a charge of 1200 coulombs flowed through the circuit, how long was the circuit switched on for?

   b) Describe the process taking place during electrolysis.

OCR Reference: Page 68 — *Lonsdale* Science Revision Guides - OCR Science: Phase 2 — 59

RESISTANCE

Using Electricity — 4

1. a) What is resistance?

b) What is the difference between a fixed and a variable resistor?

2. The circuit below was used to measure the resistance of a fixed resistor.

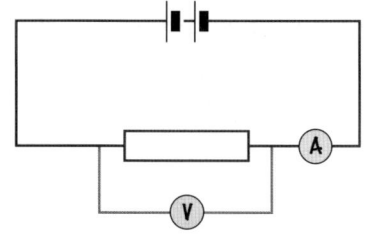

   a) If the first reading on the voltmeter is 6.0V and the ammeter is 1.5A, calculate the resistance of the resistor.

   b) What would happen to the readings on the voltmeter and ammeter if one of the cells was removed? Explain your answer.

   c) A different resistor was placed in the circuit and the current flowing when the potential difference is 6V is 0.2A. Calculate the resistance of the resistor.

---- HIGHER TIER ----

3. For the circuits shown below, each cell provides a potential difference of 1.5V. The total resistance of two resistors in series is simply their resistance added together. For each circuit calculate:

(i) [Circuit: 2 cells, A, V₁ across 2Ω, V₂ across 4Ω]
a) p.d. supplied =
b) Total resistance =
c) Ammeter reading =
d) V₁ =   V₂ =

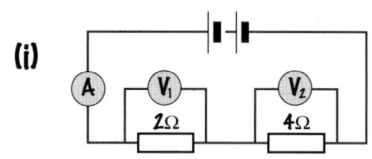

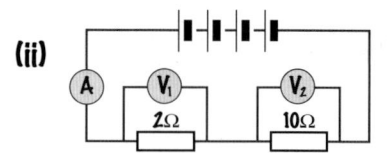

(ii) [Circuit: 4 cells, A, V₁ across 2Ω, V₂ across 10Ω]
a) p.d. supplied =
b) Total resistance =
c) Ammeter reading =
d) V₁ =   V₂ =

(iii) [Circuit: 4 cells, A, V₁ across 20Ω, V₂ across 100Ω]
a) p.d. supplied =
b) Total resistance =
c) Ammeter reading =
d) V₁ =   V₂ =

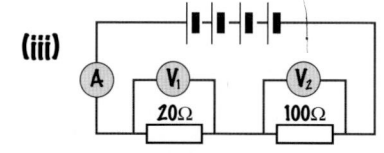

(iv) [Circuit: 2 cells, A, V₁ across 5Ω, V₂ across 10Ω]
a) p.d. supplied =
b) Total resistance =
c) Ammeter reading =
d) V₁ =   V₂ =

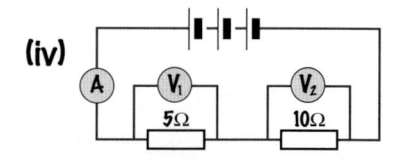

RESISTANCE OF COMPONENTS

Using Electricity — HIGHER TIER

1. Jill decides to investigate how the current flowing through a filament lamp changes with the potential difference across it. Jill obtained the results below.

POTENTIAL DIFFERENCE (V)	0.0	1.0	2.0	3.0	4.0	5.0
CURRENT (A)	0.0	1.1	1.7	2.1	2.3	2.5

a) Plot a graph of current against potential difference.

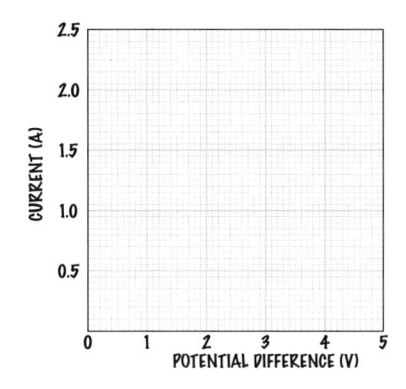

b) Explain the shape of the graph.

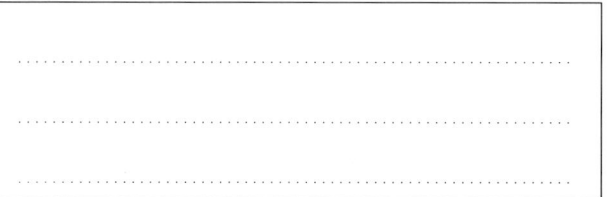

c) On the graph paper below sketch a graph of current against potential difference if a diode was used instead of a lamp.

2. The graph shows how the amount of light falling on a light dependent resistor affects its resistance.

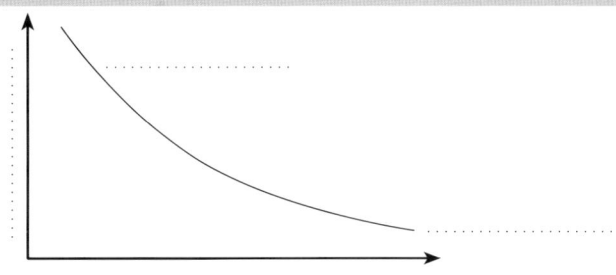

   a) Label the axes and the graph.
   b) Explain the shape of the graph.

3. Simon carried out an investigation using a thermistor. He placed the thermistor in water at different temperatures. Readings of voltage and current were taken. Here are the results.

TEMPERATURE (°C)	VOLTAGE (V)	CURRENT (A)	RESISTANCE (Ω)
20	12	1.0	
30	12	1.5	
40	12	2.1	
50	12	3.0	
60	12	4.0	
70	12	4.8	

a) Calculate the value of the resistance of the thermistor for each set of readings.

b) Use the axes below to plot a graph of resistance against temperature.

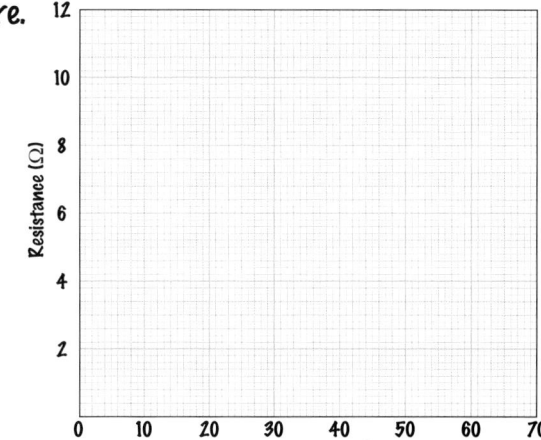

c) From your graph what was the resistance at ...

(i) 35°C .... (ii) 65°C ....

d) Calculate the current flowing through the thermistor when its temperature was 35°C.

STATIC ELECTRICITY

Using Electricity — 6

1. The picture shows Paul charging a balloon with static electricity.

   a) Explain how the balloon gains a positive charge.

   b) What charge will Paul's jumper have?

2. Clouds become charged due to very small particles of ice rubbing against each other. In thunderclouds the charge is greater than normal and lightning can occur.

   a) What is lightning?

   b) If thunder clouds gain a negative charge, explain clearly how discharge occurs.

   c) Some buildings have a lightning conductor fixed to their outside wall. This is a copper rod which rises above the highest part of the building with its lower end connected to earth. How does it protect the building from lightning?

3. Hugh did an experiment in which he charged up two polythene rods and one perspex rod by rubbing them with a cloth. The charge on the rods is shown in the diagram below.

   POLYTHENE ROD RUBBED WITH A CLOTH   PERSPEX ROD RUBBED WITH A CLOTH

   a) He then suspended one of the charged polythene rods and the charged perspex rod. The other charged polythene rod was then brought up close to the suspended rods. What would you expect to see and what can we conclude from this?

   HIGHER TIER

   b) Explain how the rods become charged.

STATIC IN REAL LIFE

Using Electricity — 7

1. Bicycles can be painted using an electrostatic paint spray. The paint is given a positive charge.

   a) What charge should the bike be given? Explain your answer.

   b) What is the advantage of using this method?

2. The following statements describe how a photocopier works.

   A ... charged impression of the plate attracts tiny specs of black powder ...

   B ... paper is heated to fix the final image ...

   C ... copying plate is electrically charged ...

   D ... powder is transferred from the plate to the paper ...

   E ... image of the page to be copied is projected onto the plate ...

   F ... charge leaks away due to light, leaving an electrostatic impression of page ...

   Rearrange the statements in order to describe how a photocopier works.

   ☐ → ☐ → ☐ → ☐ → ☐ → ☐

3. Describe in detail how a laser printer works.

4. During fuelling of planes care has to be taken to avoid dangerous electrical discharges.

   a) Explain why there could be a discharge.

   b) Explain how this discharge could be made safe.

OCR Reference: Page 72

WORK AND POWER

Applications Of Physics — 1

1. A cyclist moves along a flat road against a resistive force of 100N. If the cyclist travels 1000m calculate the work done by the cyclist.

2. Donna lifts a parcel of weight 100N onto a shelf that is 2m above the ground.

    a) Calculate the work done in lifting the parcel onto the shelf.

    b) What type of energy does the parcel gain?

3. A car is driven up a mountain pass. It gains a vertical height of 300m. The weight of the car and its passengers is 10,000N.

    a) Calculate the work done by the car against gravity.

    b) What is the gain in potential energy of the car?

4. Matt cycles a distance of 2000m against a resistive force of 150N. He travels this distance in 400s.

    a) Calculate the work done by Matt.

    b) What is Matt's power output?

5. The diagram shows a pumped storage system used to store water in a dam.

    a) Calculate the work done in pumping 10,000N of water from the lower to the upper reservoir.

    b) If it takes 10s to move 10,000N of water from the bottom to the top calculate the power output of the pump.

═══ HIGHER TIER ═══

6. The output power of a crane is 1.6kW. Calculate how long it will take to lift a load of 5,000N through a distance of 8m.

KINETIC ENERGY

Applications Of Physics — 2

1. a) What is kinetic energy?

   b) A truck of mass 2000kg and a car of mass 1000kg are travelling down a motorway at the same speed:

   (i) Which one has the greatest kinetic energy?

   (ii) Explain your answer.

   c) Two cars of the same mass are travelling down a road. Explain how one car could have more kinetic energy than the other.

2. For the following pairs of objects state which has the most kinetic energy.

   a) A car of mass 1000kg or a lorry of mass 3200kg, both moving at 10m/s.

   b) Car A of mass 1000kg moving at 15m/s or Car B of mass 1000kg moving at 10m/s.

---- HIGHER TIER ----

3. A car of mass 1000kg moves along a road at a constant speed of 20m/s. Calculate it's kinetic energy.

4. A truck of mass 32,000kg moves along a road with a speed of 10m/s. Calculate the kinetic energy of the truck.

5. A skier of mass 90kg is skiing down a hill at a speed of 15m/s. What is the kinetic energy of the skier?

6. A toy truck of mass 1300g is moving at a speed of 30cm/s. Calculate its kinetic energy

7. The kinetic energy of a cyclist moving along a road is 5000J. If the mass of the cyclist is 100kg calculate the speed of the cyclist.

GRAVITATIONAL POTENTIAL ENERGY

Applications Of Physics — 3

1. a) What is gravitational potential energy?

   b) Give TWO examples of an object that has gravitational potential energy.
   (i) .... (ii) ....

2. The diagram shows a bungee jumper, at various stages.

   a) Which type of energy does the jumper have at the top of the jump, (diagram (A))

   b) Which types of energy does the jumper have when falling down? (diagram (B))

   c) If two people, John of mass 60kg and Jill of mass 80kg, were doing the jump, which would have the most energy at the top?

---- HIGHER TIER ----

3. A cyclist climbs from a height of 100m to a height of 300m. The mass of the cyclist is 70kg.

   By how much does the gravitational potential energy of the cyclist increase? (remember: formula, working and unit).

4. An electric motor of power rating 4000W lifts a load of 400N. It takes 10s to lift the load.

   a) What is the main energy change taking place?

   b) If the motor is 100% efficient how much energy does the motor transfer to the load? (remember formula, working and unit).

   c) What is the gain in gravitational potential energy of the load?

   d) What height is the load lifted through? (remember: formula, working and unit).

5. The diagram shows a diver. The mass of the diver is 70kg. The gravitational field strength is 10N/Kg.

   Calculate the speed of the diver on entry to the pool.

   3.2m

ELECTRIC MOTORS

Applications Of Physics — 4

1. a) The diagram shows a piece of wire in a magnetic field. Describe what happens when the current is switched on. What is the name given to this effect?

b) What energy transfer takes place when the current is switched on?

HIGHER TIER

2. a) A direct current (d.c.) motor uses the motor effect. When a current flows through the coil side A moves down. Why does side B move up?

b) What would happen to the rotation if the current were reversed?

c) Explain simply how the motor works.

d) What would happen if a.c. and not d.c. were used?

e) The circuit shown can be used to control the motor in a remote controlled toy car. All cells are identical. With switch B closed and switch A open the car moves forward.

  (i) What would happen to the car if switch B is opened and switch A is closed? Explain your answer.

  (ii) In which direction does the car travel the fastest? Explain your answer.

  (iii) What would happen to the car if both switches were closed? Explain your answer.

PRODUCTION AND DISTRIBUTION OF ELECTRICITY

Applications Of Physics — 5

1. The diagram shows how electricity is generated in a fossil fuel power station.

   a) Describe the process by which electricity is produced by burning coal.

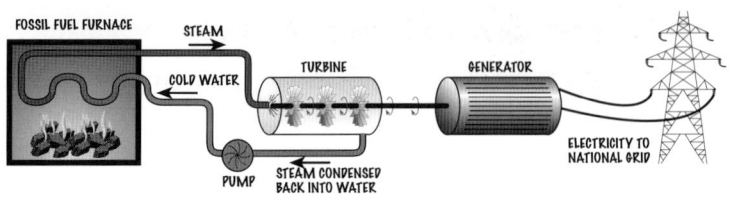

   b) What happens to the wasted energy during this process?

   c) The diagram below shows what happens to every 100 joules of chemical energy we have at the beginning of the production process.

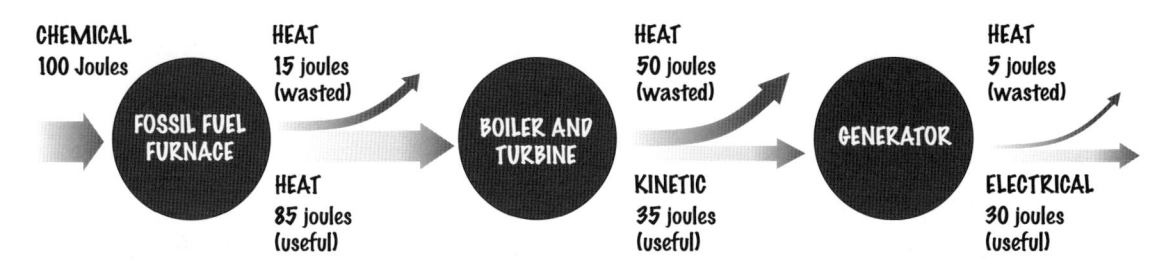

   Complete the table below to work out the efficiency at each stage.

STAGE	USEFUL OUTPUT (J)	INPUT (J)	% EFFICIENCY
FOSSIL FUEL FURNACE			
BOILER AND TURBINE			
GENERATOR			

2. The diagram shows a system called the National Grid used for transmitting electricity all over the country.

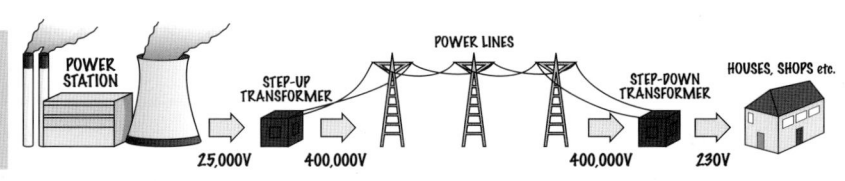

   Describe the use of transformers in the National Grid.

GENERATORS AND TRANSFORMERS

Applications Of Physics — 6

1. The diagram shows a bicycle dynamo.

   a) Explain how the dynamo makes a lamp light on the bike.

   b) Why is it more dangerous to have your bike lights powered by a dynamo rather than batteries when going slowly uphill in the dark?

2. a) The diagram shows a transformer. Name the material used to make the core of the transformer.

   b) Is this a step-up or step-down transformer?

   c) Explain fully how a transformer works.

   — HIGHER TIER —

   d) Electricity could be transmitted at a high voltage and a low current or at a low voltage and a high current. Explain how we transmit electricity and why we do it this way.

3. A transformer can step-up or step-down a voltage. Complete the table below.

VOLTAGE ACROSS PRIMARY	VOLTAGE ACROSS SECONDARY	NUMBER OF TURNS ON PRIMARY	NUMBER OF TURNS ON SECONDARY	STEP-UP OR STEP-DOWN?
12V	240V	100		
400,000V	200V		1,000	
25,000V		20,000	20	
	230V	150	1,500	

4. A small transformer has a primary coil of 100 turns and a secondary coil of 500 turns.

   a) Is it a step-up or step-down transformer?

   b) The current flowing through the primary coil of the transformer is 0.5A when it is connected to a 24V a.c supply. (i) Calculate the power delivered to the primary coil.

   (ii) If the transformer is 100% efficient what is the power output from the secondary coil?

   (iii) What voltage would the secondary coil produce?

ELECTROMAGNETIC WAVES

Applications Of Physics — 7

1. a) Which type(s) of electromagnetic wave is used for ...

i) Radar ....

ii) Optical information ....

iii) Broadcasting of TV programmes ....

iv) Remote control for TV ....

v) Satellite communication ....

vi) Telecommunications through optical fibres ....

b) Name three things that the above electromagnetic waves have in common.

i) ....

ii) ....

iii) ....

2. a) The diagram shows a length of optical fibre.

b) Explain why a ray of light or infra-red is totally internally reflected along its length and not refracted.

....

---- HIGHER TIER ----

3. An endoscope is an instrument which can be used by a doctor to see inside the human body. The instrument uses optical fibres.

Explain, using the diagram to help you if you wish, how the endoscope works.

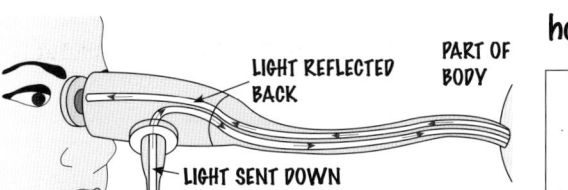

....

4. a) Explain how satellites can be used for communication.

....

b) Explain how the ionosphere can be used for communication.

....

c) Explain how refraction and diffraction of electromagnetic waves can affect communications.

....

ANALOGUE AND DIGITAL SIGNALS

Applications Of Physics — 8

1. a) What are analogue signals?

   b) Name three analogue devices.
      i)   ii)   iii)

   c) What are digital signals?

   d) Name three digital devices.
      i)   ii)   iii)

---- HIGHER TIER ----

2. a) What are the advantages of using digital signals instead of analogue signals?

   b) What is multiplexing?

   c) i) What problems are there in transferring data from one computer to another computer using a phone line?

      ii) Explain, using diagrams to help you, how this problem is overcome.

OCR Reference: Page 81

SPEED, VELOCITY AND ACCELERATION

Earth, Space And Nuclear Radiation — 1

1. The car in the diagram is travelling at a constant 50km/h.

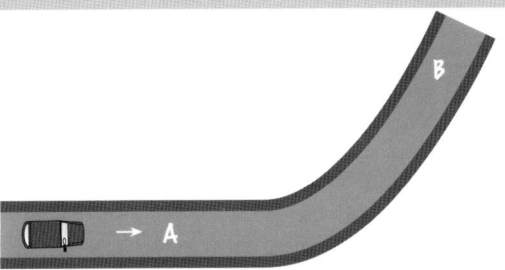

   a) Does the speed of the car change as it goes from A to B? Explain your answer.

   b) Does the velocity of the car change as it goes from A to B? Explain your answer.

2. The data below shows part of a bus journey. Use the data to draw a velocity-time graph for the journey.

Time(s)	0	10	20	30	40	50	60	70	80	90	100	110	120
Velocity (m/s)	0	5	10	15	15	15	20	20	20	15	15	7.5	0

   a) Between which two times was the bus's acceleration the greatest?

   b) Calculate the acceleration of the bus during the two times.

   c) Calculate the deceleration of the bus.

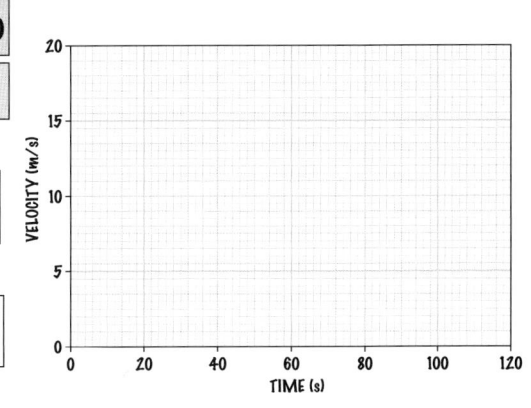

3. A cyclist at the top of a hill has a speed of 4m/s. 10 seconds later his speed is 10m/s. Calculate the acceleration of the cyclist.

HIGHER TIER

4. Complete the following table.

INITIAL VELOCITY	FINAL VELOCITY	TIME TAKEN	ACCELERATION
0m/s		12s	1.5m/s^2
24m/s	10m/s	5s	
	14m/s	10s	-0.5m/s^2
80cm/s	1.2m/s	0.5s	
2m/s	20m/s		1.8m/s^2
	25m/s	4 minutes	0.1m/s^2

TERMINAL SPEED

Earth, Space And Nuclear Radiation — 2

1. The drawing shows a skydiver of weight 700N who has just stepped out of a plane.

   a) Why does the skydiver fall?

   b) What happens to the weight of the skydiver as she falls?

   c) Eventually the skydiver will fall with a steady speed. Explain in terms of the forces acting on the skydiver why she falls with a steady speed.

--- HIGHER TIER ---

2. a) When the skydiver above steps out of the plane she initially accelerates. Explain in terms of the forces acting on the skydiver, why she accelerates.

   b) What will happen to the value of the air resistance as she falls? Why does this happen?

   c) Eventually, after she has reached terminal speed, the skydiver opens her parachute. What effect will this have on the air resistance acting on her?

   d) What will happen to the speed of the skydiver now?

   e) Eventually the skydiver will stop decelerating. Explain why.

3. The table below shows the speed of a skydiver at 5 second intervals after he steps out of a plane up to the point where he opens his parachute.

Speed (m/s)	0	10	19	27	33	36	38	39	40	40	40
Time (s)	0	5	10	15	20	25	30	35	40	45	50

   a) Draw a speed-time graph of the falling skydiver on the axes opposite.

   b) The skydiver eventually comes to rest on the ground after 78s. On the axes opposite complete the graph, showing how his speed might change after 50s.

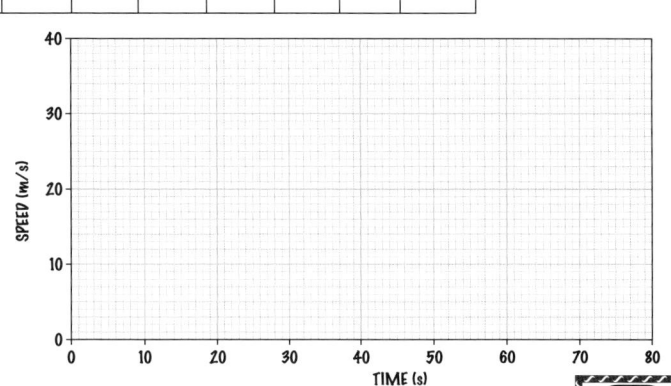

OCR Reference: Page 84

FORCES IN ACTION

Earth, Space And Nuclear Radiation — 3

HIGHER TIER

1. a) The diagrams show the forces acting on a moving car of mass 1200kg going from left to right. For each diagram calculate the acceleration of the car.

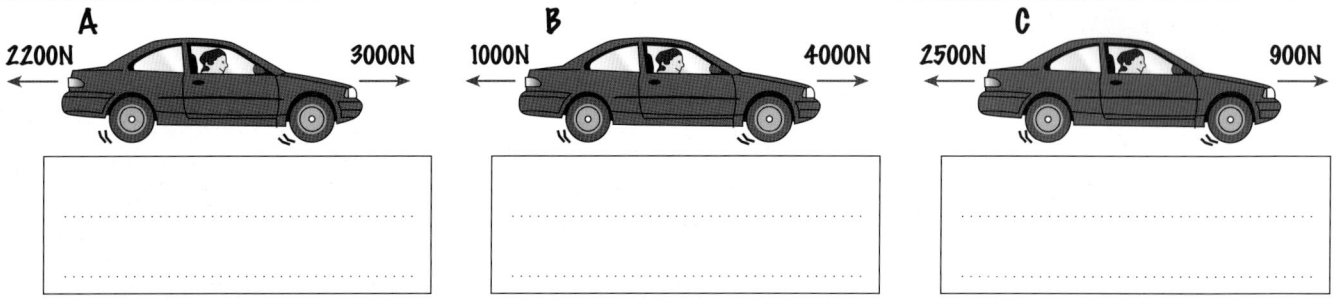

A ← 2200N car 3000N →

B ← 1000N car 4000N →

C ← 2500N car 900N →

b) The cars in the following diagrams are all moving from left to right. The mass of each car is 1200kg. For each car calculate the value of the missing force.

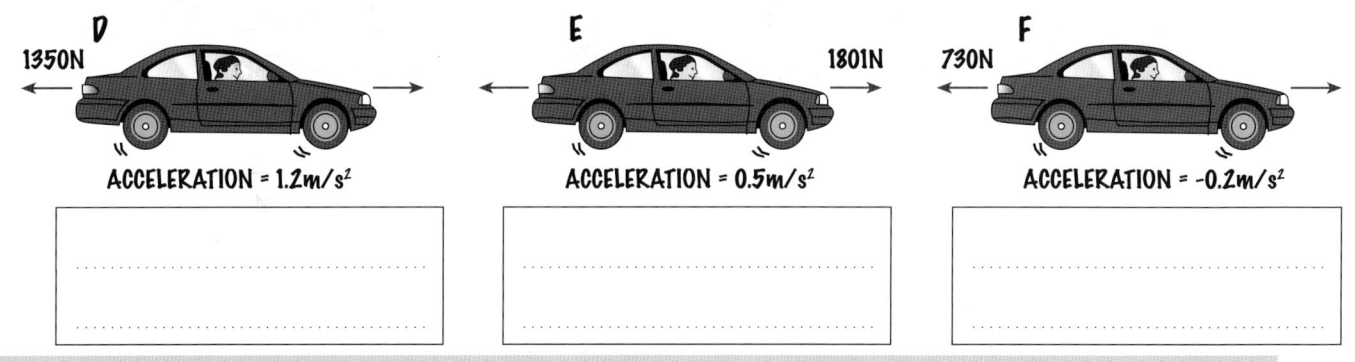

D ← 1350N car → ?   ACCELERATION = 1.2m/s²

E ← ? car 1801N →   ACCELERATION = 0.5m/s²

F ← 730N car → ?   ACCELERATION = -0.2m/s²

2. a) A number of masses are shown below. Calculate their weight on Earth. (g=10m/s² or 10N/kg)

   (i) Mass = 2kg;
   (ii) Mass = 10kg;
   (iii) Mass = 250g;
   (iv) Mass = 75g;

   b) A number of weights are shown below. Calculate their mass. (g=10m/s² or 10N/kg)

   (i) Weight = 250N;
   (ii) Weight = 25N;
   (iii) Weight = 4.5N;
   (iv) Weight = 8N;

   c) On the Moon every 1kg of matter has a weight of 1.7N. An object on the Moon has a weight of 340N. Calculate its weight on Earth.

3. Explain, using an example, the practical importance of the following statement. 'When body A exerts a force on body B, then body B exerts an equal but opposite force on body A.'

THE SOLAR SYSTEM

Earth, Space And Nuclear Radiation — 4

1. The diagram below shows the solar system.

   a) Six planets have not been named, write their names in the boxes provided.

1.	2.	3.

   (Diagram: SUN — 1. — VENUS — 2. — 3. — 4. — SATURN — 5. — 6. — PLUTO)

4.	5.	6.

   b) The further away an orbiting body is, the longer it takes to make a complete orbit. Name two planets which have a shorter period of orbit around the Sun compared to the Earth.

   (i) .... (ii) ....

   c) Venus is often seen to be shining in the early evening sky. Why can we see Venus?

   ....

2. The diagram shows the path of a comet around the Sun

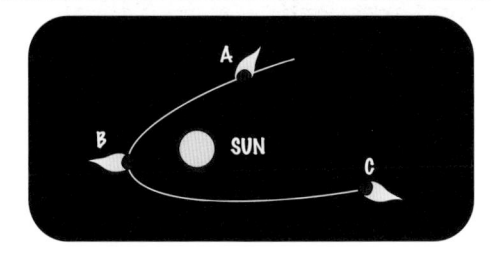

   a) What is a comet made from?

   ....

   b) Explain why the comet has a tail.

   ....

   c) Explain why comets are not seen very often.

   ....

   d) What is a meteor made from? ....

   e) Explain why a meteor can be seen when it enters the Earth's atmosphere.

   ....

HIGHER TIER

3. a) What is the name of the inward pull force provided by gravity that enables an object to stay in orbit around a larger object?

   ....

   b) Which natural object orbits the Earth because of this inward pull force? ....

   c) Which man-made objects orbit the Earth because of this inward pull force?

   ....

THE UNIVERSE

Earth, Space And Nuclear Radiation — 5

1. a) What is a star?

   b) What is a galaxy?

   c) What is a black hole?

   d) Rewrite the following in order of size, starting with the smallest:
      UNIVERSE, PLANET, GALAXY, SOLAR SYSTEM, STAR

   e) i) The distance from the Earth to the nearest star or galaxy can be measured in light years.

      What is a light year?

      ii) Why are these distances measured in light years?

2. a) What is the 'Big Bang' theory concerning the origin of the Universe?

   HIGHER TIER

   b) Why does the future of the Universe depend on the amount of mass present?

3. The picture shows a spectra from our sun and two other different stars.

   Each of the lines represent a particular wavelength.

   a) What does the spectrum of star A tell us about its movement?

   b) What does the spectrum of star B tell us about its movement?

   c) Explain how the evidence from the spectra above supports the 'Big Bang' theory of the origin of the Universe.

   d) What other piece of evidence is there that supports the 'Big Bang' theory of the origin of the Universe.

THE LIFE HISTORY OF A STAR

Earth, Space And Nuclear Radiation — 6

HIGHER TIER

1. a) Describe, in as much detail as possible, how stars like our Sun were formed.

   b) (i) Our Sun is currently going through a stable period in its life cycle. What is it called during this period?

   (ii) Describe the forces at work in the Sun during this stable period.

2. a) The two flow diagrams show the cycle of change which occurs when a star dies. Each circle shows what is formed at the end of each change. Complete each circle in the cycle by using the following words.

   NEUTRON STAR   SUPERNOVA   WHITE DWARF   PLANETARY NEBULA   RED GIANT

   STAR → ○ → (For medium-weight stars) → ○ → Stage A → ○

   STAR → ○ → (For heavy-weight stars) → ○ → Stage B → ○

   → Stage C → BLACK HOLE

   b) Explain what happens during stage A.

   c) Explain what happens during stage B.

   d) Explain what happens during stage C.

LIFE IN THE UNIVERSE

Earth, Space And Nuclear Radiation — 7

1. a) Why have scientists for a long time recognised that there is the possibility of life elsewhere in the Universe?

   b) There are many ways of obtaining evidence that life does exist in other places in our Solar System. Explain the disadvantages of obtaining evidence by the following methods.

   (i) Actually travelling there in order to look for signs of life.

   (ii) Using robots to travel there in order to bring back samples.

   (iii) Using robots to travel there in order to take pictures.

   (iv) Using radio telescopes to detect radio messages.

2. Mars and Europa (one of Jupiter's satellites) are amongst the prime contenders for life in our solar system. Name four conditions that are probably necessary for life to exist.

   (i) .... (iii) ....
   (ii) .... (iv) ....

HIGHER TIER

3. a) Describe how a sample of a meteorite can be analysed to detect the existence of life.

   b) Why do you think that the search for extra-terrestrial intelligence (SETI) using radio telescopes has so far been unsuccessful in detecting life elsewhere in the Universe?

   c) A star has been observed to have a very small 'wobble'. What can we conclude from this?

NUCLEAR RADIATION

Earth, Space And Nuclear Radiation — 8

1. What do we mean if we say a substance is radioactive?

   ....

2. a) Below are the three types of radiation and a list of descriptions. Match the radiation to the correct description with an arrow (a description can apply to more than one ionising radiation).

   | α |
   | β |
   | γ |

   - Emitted from the nucleus.
   - Passes through air and paper but absorbed by a few mm of aluminium.
   - Very high frequency radiation.
   - Consists of two protons and two neutrons.
   - Very short wavelength radiation.
   - Fast moving electron.
   - Absorbed by a thin sheet of paper.
   - Has a positive charge.
   - Helium nucleus.

   b) Why does the emission of gamma radiation have no effect on the structure of the nucleus?

   ....

3. The data below shows the dose of radiation received from certain sources of radiation in one year by a person living in the UK.

   a) Complete the table.

Source of Radiation	Dose received (arbitrary units)	Percentage of Total Dose received
Food	0.24	
Rocks and Soil	0.30	
Cosmic Radiation	0.20	
Medical	0.16	
Air	1.10	
	Total =	

   b) Draw a pie chart to display the data.

   c) What percentage of the total dose received comes from natural sources?

   ....

BENEFICIAL AND HARMFUL EFFECTS OF NUCLEAR RADIATION
Earth, Space And Nuclear Radiation — 9

1. a) The diagram below shows a simple smoke detector. Explain what happens when α particles pass between the two electrodes.

   b) Explain what subsequently happens if smoke enters the space between the two electrodes.

2. The diagram shows a method of controlling the thickness of steel at a steel mill. A radioactive source which emits γ rays is placed on one side of the steel and a radiation detector is placed on the other.

   a) How will the amount of radiation reaching the detector change as the steel gets thicker?

   b) What effect will this have on the distance between the rollers?

   c) Explain, in detail, why a radioisotope which emits α or β particles could not be used for this job

   d) Explain, in detail, why a radioisotope which emits γ rays is used for this job.

3. Radiation can be used to sterilise medical instruments.

   a) What type of radiation would be used for this job?

   b) Why do the instruments become sterile?

   c) What is the advantage of sterilising the instruments in this way compared to heating or chemical treatment?

4. Radiation emitted from a radioactive material is often called 'ionising radiation.'

   a) Explain what is meant by the word 'ionising'.

   b) Why is ionising radiation dangerous to humans?